English File

student's book

1

D0177334

OXFORD UNIVERSITY PRESS

Paul Seligson and Clive Oxenden are the original co-authors of
English File 1 (pub. 1996) and *English File 2* (pub. 1997).

Progress chart

Contents · Grammar · Vocabulary

Contents	*Grammar*	*Vocabulary*

Key to symbols

🛄 = Travel with English Travel phrasebook	🎲 = Game
◁▷ = Revision and extension	Ⓥ = Vocabulary file
🔍 = Focus on …	Ⓖ = Grammar file
	☑ = Check your progress
►◄ = Communication	
⌐ = Listening	
✎ = Word bank	

At the airport

> *Hello. I'm Sophie.*
> *Hi! I'm Mike. Nice to meet you.*

1 **a** ○ **1** ○ Listen. Number the photos 1 to 4.

1 **MIKE** Excuse me?
   WOMAN Yes?
   MIKE Are you Sophie Villeneuve?
   WOMAN No, I'm not.
   MIKE Sorry.

2 **MIKE** Excuse me, are you Sophie Villeneuve?
   SOPHIE Yes, I am.

3 **MIKE** Hi, I'm Mike. Mike North. Nice to meet you.
   SOPHIE Hello. Nice to meet you.
   MIKE Welcome to Dublin.
   SOPHIE Thank you.

4 **MIKE** Bye! See you tomorrow.
   SOPHIE Goodbye. And thanks.

b Listen again and repeat. Practise in pairs.

GRAMMAR FOCUS

Verb *be*: *I / you*

+ Positive	− Negative
I'm Mike.	I'm not Mike.
You're Sophie.	You aren't Sophie.

? Question	✓✗ Short answer
Are you Sophie?	Yes, I am. NOT ~~Yes, I'm.~~
	No, I'm not.

Contractions   'm = am   're = are   aren't = are not

I Tarzan. You Jane.

No! I'm Tarzan. You're Jane.

PRACTICE

Practise in pairs.

A Hello. I'm …
B Hi! I'm … Nice to meet you.
A Are you …?
B No, I'm not. I'm …

2 **a** Write the numbers.

four ~~one~~ eight two ten six

1 *one*	6 _____
2 _____	7 seven
3 three	8 _____
4 _____	9 nine
5 five	10 _____

b ◦ 2 ◦ Listen. Repeat the numbers.

c ◦ 3 ◦ Listen. Write the numbers.

3 **a** ◦ 4 ◦ Match the words and pictures 1 to 6. Listen and repeat.

<u>car</u> park [6]   <u>tele</u>phones [ ]   infor<u>ma</u>tion [ ]
<u>ta</u>xis [ ]   <u>toi</u>lets [ ]   <u>res</u>taurant [ ]

PRONUNCIATION

a ◦ 5 ◦ Listen and repeat.

I   Hi!   nice   five   nine   Bye!

me   meet   I'm   number   tomorrow   welcome

b ◦ 6 ◦ Listen. Underline the stress.

1 computer	6 shampoo
2 television	7 banana
3 football	8 video camera
4 university	9 hotel
5 cinema	10 airport

4 Write six 'international' English words. Underline the stress.

*ham*burger
*cof*fee

tennis

radio

Hello. / Hi!   **Ⓥ**
Goodbye. / Bye!
See you (tomorrow)!

b Test a partner.

A Number 5?
B Toilets. Number 3?

❶ ☎   ❷ ⓘ   ❸ 🚕   ❹ 🍴   ❺ 🚻   ❻ P

At the reception desk

What's your name?
How do you spell it?

PRONUNCIATION

a ° 7 ° Listen. Repeat the words, sounds, and letters.

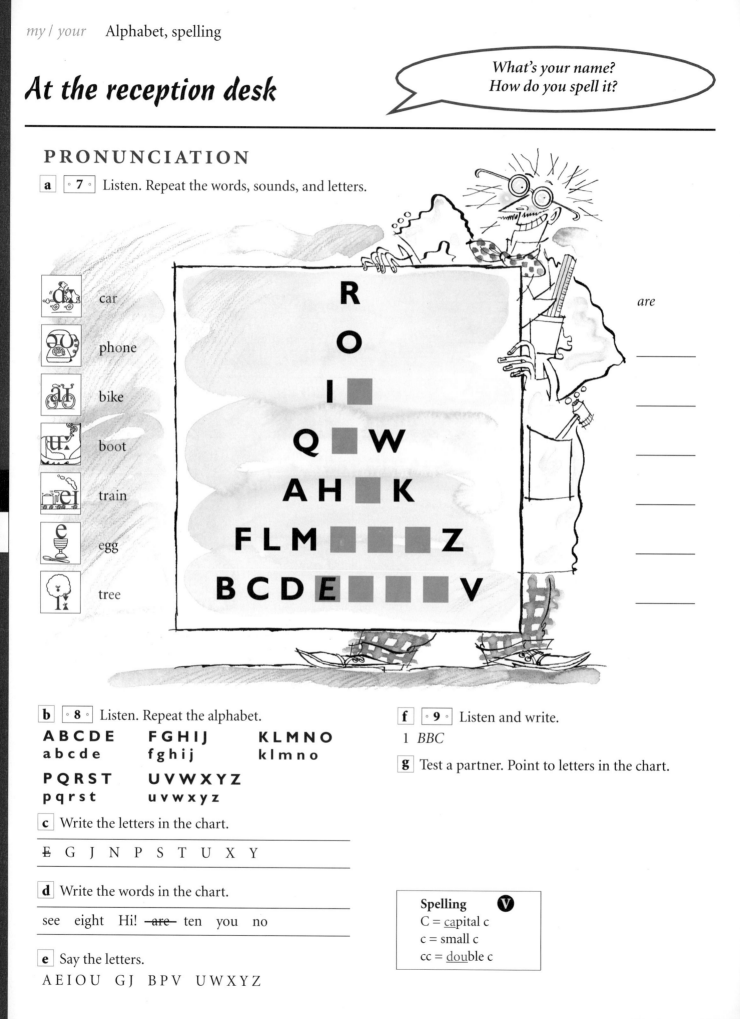

car

phone

bike

boot

train

egg

tree

are

1

B

b ° 8 ° Listen. Repeat the alphabet.

A B C D E   **F G H I J**   **K L M N O**
a b c d e   f g h i j   k l m n o

P Q R S T   **U V W X Y Z**
p q r s t   u v w x y z

c Write the letters in the chart.

E̶ G J N P S T U X Y

d Write the words in the chart.

see   eight   Hi!   a̶r̶e̶   ten   you   no

e Say the letters.

A E I O U   G J   B P V   U W X Y Z

f ° 9 ° Listen and write.

1 *BBC*

g Test a partner. Point to letters in the chart.

Spelling 🅥
C = <u>capital</u> c
c = small c
cc = <u>double</u> c

6

1 ◦**10**◦ Listen. Complete the form.

The Red House Conference Centre

Surname ___VILL___

First name ___SO___

Room number ___

Good morning	=	to `12 : 00`	**V**
Good afternoon	=	`12 : 00` to `18 : 00`	
Good evening	=	`18 : 00` to `24 : 00`	
Goodnight	=		

RECEPTIONIST Good evening. What's your name, please?

SOPHIE ▓▓▓▓▓▓▓.

RECEPTIONIST Sorry?

SOPHIE My name's ▓▓▓▓▓▓▓.

RECEPTIONIST How do you spell it?

SOPHIE ▓▓▓▓▓▓▓.

RECEPTIONIST ▓▓▓▓▓▓▓.

SOPHIE Yes, that's right.

RECEPTIONIST And your first name?

SOPHIE ▓▓▓▓▓. That's ▓▓▓▓▓.

RECEPTIONIST Where are you from?

SOPHIE ▓▓▓▓, in ▓▓▓▓▓.

RECEPTIONIST OK. Thank you. You're in room ▓▓▓▓.

3 **a** ◦**11**◦ Listen to two people at the reception desk. Complete the forms.

① *The Red House* Conference Centre

Surname ___

First name ___DIETER___

Room number ___

② *The Red House* Conference Centre

Surname ___

First name ___

Room number ___

b Role-play with different names.

Good morning, etc.	Hi! / Hello. **V**
My name's Sophie.	I'm Sophie.
Thank you.	Thanks.
Goodbye.	Bye!

2 **a** Listen again and repeat.

b Practise with your name and country.

Contractions What's = What is
My name's = My name is

1

B

7

Who's famous?

1 Point and ask with photos A to H.

  A What's her name?
  B Sophia Loren. / I don't know. What's his name?

2 **a** Write the words in the chart.

France Brazil Egyptian German ~~Italian~~
Japan Poland Spanish

	Country	**Nationality**
	Italy	*Italian*
	_____	Polish
	Germany	_____
	_____	Japanese
	Spain	_____
	_____	French
	Egypt	_____
	_____	Brazilian

b ° **12** ° Listen. Who is it (A to H)?

1 She's from Italy. She's Italian. = *E Sophia Loren*

c Listen again. <u>Underline</u> the stress on the words in the chart.

I<u>ta</u>ly I<u>ta</u>lian

3 **a** Test a partner. Point and ask.

  A What's his name?
  B Pele.
  A Where's he from?
  B He's from Brazil. What's …?

b ✎ **Countries, nationalities, and languages** *p.132*
Where are you from? What nationality are you?

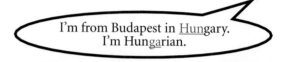

DIETER Hi! I'm Dieter.
SOPHIE Hello. I'm Sophie. Nice to meet you.
DIETER This is Mona. She's E_____ .
SOPHIE Hi, Mona.
MONA Hello. Nice to meet you.
SOPHIE Where are you from in E_____ ?
MONA Alexandria.

SOPHIE Is Dieter A_____ ?
MONA No, he isn't. He's G_____ . I think he's from Hamburg.

1
C

4 **a** ⌈°13°⌉ Listen. Where are Mona and Dieter from?

b Listen again. Complete the dialogue.

c Role-play in threes. **A** You're Dieter. **B** You're Mona. **C** You're Sophie.

d Role-play with famous names.

GRAMMAR FOCUS

Verb *be*: *he* / *she*

● Use *he* for a man . Use *she* for a woman .

+		−	
He's She's Sophie's	French.	He She Sophie	isn't German.

?		✓ ✗
Is	he she Sophie	Italian?	Yes, he / she **is**. NOT ~~Yes, he's.~~ No, he / she **isn't**.

Contractions	's = is isn't = is not

Possessive adjectives: *my* / *your* / *his* / *her*

I	→	my	*My* name's Dieter.
you	→	your	Is *your* name Mona?
he	→	his	*His* name's Julio Iglesias.
she	→	her	*Her* name's Catherine Deneuve.

● Write *his* or *her*.

Use _____ for a man.

Use _____ for a woman.

PRACTICE

Complete the sentences.

1 He's from Germany. His name's Dieter. He's *German.*

2 She's from Egypt. Her name's _____. She's

_____.

3 _____ _____ France. _____

_____ Sophie. _____ _____.

4 _____ _____ _____. _____

_____ Julio Iglesias. _____ _____.

PRONUNCIATION

a ⌈°14°⌉ Listen and repeat.

yes   ten   spell   French   seven   letter

no   not   name   morning   Spanish   German

b ⌈°15°⌉ Listen and repeat.

1 Where's she from?
2 Where's he from?
3 What's his name?
4 What's her name?
5 Is she Japanese?
6 Is he from Milan?
7 His name's Tim.
8 Her name's Helena.

5 ►◄ Famous names? **A** *p.118* **B** *p.121*

6 **a** Test a partner. Point to other students.
What's her name? Where's he from? Is she from …?

b Write about you and three other students.
I'm Anna Maria. I'm from Perugia in Italy. Susanne's …

1

C

Classroom communication

> *What's this in English?*
> *It's a ...*

Important phone numbers

🔑	Reception	00
☎	Operator	01
🚕	Taxis	682471
✈	Airport	799426
🚆	Station	481332
ℹ	Tourist information	547692

STUDENT
Excuse me, please.
What's this in English?
How do you spell it?
How do you pronounce it?
Thank you.

TEACHER
C-A-double S-E-double T-E.
Ca<u>ss</u>ette.
It's 'a cassette'.
Yes?

1 **a** °**16**° Listen. How do you say [cassette] in English?

  b Listen again. Match the questions and answers.

2 **a** Match the words and pictures A to J.

a door	*I*	a <u>pen</u>cil	☐	a <u>vi</u>deo	☐
a <u>win</u>dow	☐	a <u>piece</u> of <u>paper</u>	☐	a bag	☐
a book	☐	a desk	☐		
a pen	☐	a chair	☐		

b Practise the dialogue. Ask the teacher questions about pictures K to P.
What's picture K in English?

c Test a partner. Point to pictures.
  A What's this in English?
  B It's 'a book'. / I don't remember.
  A How do you spell it?

1
D

GRAMMAR FOCUS

Verb *be*: *it*

+	−
It's a cassette.	It isn't a cassette.
?	✓ ✗
Is it a cassette?	Yes, it is. / No, it isn't.

● Use *it* for a thing.

3 Play *Guess the picture.* **A** Choose a picture. **B** Guess it in ten questions.

  B Is it a chair?
  A Yes, it is. / No, it isn't.

4 Match the words and pictures Q to X.

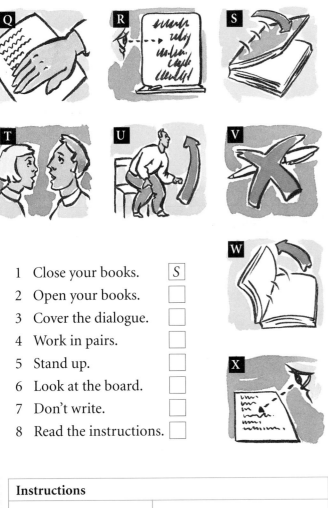

1 Close your books.	S	
2 Open your books.		
3 Cover the dialogue.		
4 Work in pairs.		
5 Stand up.		
6 Look at the board.		
7 Don't write.		
8 Read the instructions.		

Instructions	
+	−
Sit down.	Don't write.
Open your books.	Don't look at your books.

● Say *please* to be polite.
  Open your books, **please**.

5 What are 1 to 5 in your country?

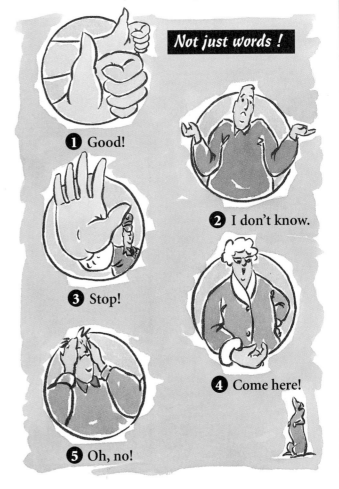

Not just words !

❶ Good!
❷ I don't know.
❸ Stop!
❹ Come here!
❺ Oh, no!

◦ 17 ◦ Listen and repeat.

K	come book desk classroom contraction question
🐟	it in is sit this window listen dictionary

Phone numbers   **V**
0 = oh /əʊ/
44 = double four
444 = four double four

6 **a** **◦ 18 ◦** Listen and check the **Important phone numbers** on page 10. Right ✓ or wrong ✗ ?

  b Say the phone numbers.

  1   01857 880462
  2   0171 633 2265
  3   01341 99007

  c ▶◀ **Phone numbers** A *p.118* B *p.121*

In the conference room

Are you German?
No, we aren't.

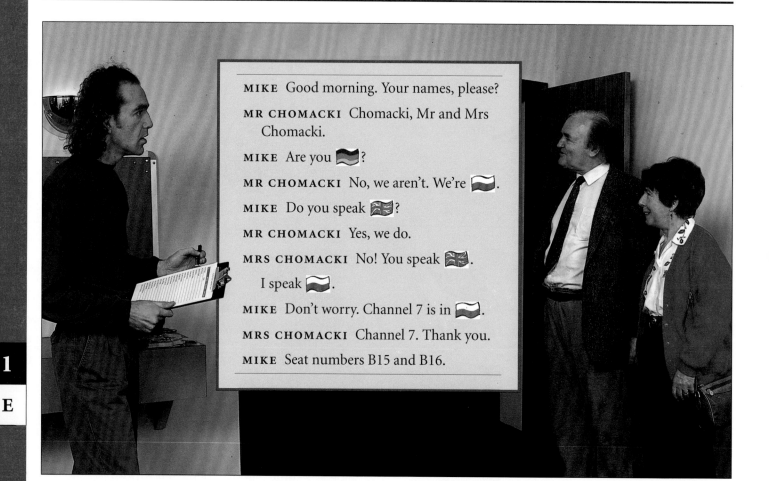

MIKE Good morning. Your names, please?

MR CHOMACKI Chomacki, Mr and Mrs Chomacki.

MIKE Are you 🏴？

MR CHOMACKI No, we aren't. We're 🏴.

MIKE Do you speak 🏴？

MR CHOMACKI Yes, we do.

MRS CHOMACKI No! You speak 🏴.
I speak 🏴.

MIKE Don't worry. Channel 7 is in 🏴.

MRS CHOMACKI Channel 7. Thank you.

MIKE Seat numbers B15 and B16.

1 [a] Complete the numbers.

11	12	13	14
e*le*ven	*twelve*	_ _irteen	_ _urteen

15	16	17	18
_ _fteen	_ _xteen	_ _venteen	_ _ghteen

19	20	21
_ _neteen	_ _enty	_ _enty-one

[b] °19° Listen. <u>Underline</u> the stress.

[c] °20° Write numbers 22 to 29. Remember the hyphen (-). Listen and repeat.
twenty-two

°21° Listen and repeat.

  we   three   read   speak   please   fifteen

2 [a] °22° Listen. Right ✓ or wrong ✗?

1 Mr and Mrs Chomacki are German. ☐

2 Mrs Chomacki speaks English. ☐

3 Channel 7 is in German. ☐

[b] Complete the chart for Mr and Mrs Chomacki.

The Red House **Conference Centre**

Name	Nationality	Speak English?	Seat number
Mr Chomacki	*Polish*		} /
Mrs Chomacki			
Russell Di Napoli			
Ana Martin			
Mr and Mrs Otawa			/

[c] °23° Listen. Complete the chart.

[d] Practise the dialogue in threes.

GRAMMAR FOCUS

Verb *be*: *we / you / they*

● Complete the chart.

Singular		Plural	
+	**−**	**+**	**−**
I'm	I'm not	_____'re	we aren't
_____'re	_____ aren't	you're	you _____
he's _____'s it's	he _____ isn't it	they're	_____ aren't

PRACTICE

Complete the sentences.

1 I'*m* English. Y_____'re German.
2 He _____n't Polish. He'_____ Brazilian.
3 '_____ you British?' 'No, _____'m not. I'_____ American.'
4 We'_____ from Italy. Where _____ you from?
5 '_____ they Egyptian?' 'No, they _____ .
   They'_____ French.'
6 '_____ you from Hungary?' 'Yes, we _____ .'

PRONUNCIATION

°24° Listen and repeat.

1 Is he <u>Spa</u>nish? <u>No</u>, he <u>isn't</u>. He <u>isn't</u> <u>Spa</u>nish. He's <u>It</u>alian.
2 Is she <u>French</u>? <u>Yes</u>, she <u>is</u>. She's <u>French</u>.
3 Are you <u>Ger</u>man? <u>Yes</u>, we <u>are</u>. We're <u>Ger</u>man.
4 Are you <u>Eng</u>lish? <u>No</u>, I'm <u>not</u>. I'm <u>not</u> <u>Eng</u>lish. I'm <u>I</u>rish.

3 ▶◀ **Questions and answers A** *p.118* **B** *p.121*

4 **a** °25° Listen. Repeat the days. <u>Underline</u> the stress.

The Red House Conference Centre

Conference programme			
	Morning	Afternoon	Evening
<u>Sunday</u>		Check-in	Cocktail party
Monday	Opening ceremony	Talks	Conference dinner
Tuesday	Free	Talks	Dinner (Chinese restaurant)
Wednesday	Talks	Tour of Dublin	Concert (National Concert Hall)
Thursday	Talks	Free	Disco
Friday	Talks	Closing ceremony	Goodbye party
Saturday	Check-out		

b Answer the questions.

1 When's the conference dinner?
   It's on Monday evening.
2 When's the tour of Dublin?
3 When's the disco?
4 When's the closing ceremony?
5 When's the goodbye party?
6 When are they free?

5 °26° Listen. Point to the right picture.

Not just words!

❶ happy ❷ sad ❸ angry ❹ bored

1

E

13

On the plane

TRAVEL WITH ENGLISH

SAM	Good *morning*. Anything to drink, sir?
JOE	Sorry?
SAM	Orange juice? Coke? Mineral water?
JOE	✗ _____, thank you. Nothing for me.
SAM	'Madam' ? And for you, madam?
KEIKO	_____ _____, please.
SAM	Ice and lemon?
KEIKO	✔ _____, please.
SAM	Here you are.
KEIKO	Thanks.
SAM	'Sir' ? And for you, sir?
IVAN	_____, please.
SAM	Milk and sugar?
IVAN	✔ ✗ _____, no _____.
SAM	Here you are.
IVAN	Thank you very much.
SAM	You're welcome.

1 Match the words and pictures A to J.

orange juice	*B*	coke		
mineral water		ice		
lemon		milk		
tea		coffee		
sugar		flight attendant		

2 **a** ° 27 ° Listen. Number in order (1 to 3).

Mineral water with ice and lemon. ☐

Nothing. *1*

White coffee, no sugar. ☐

b Listen again and complete the dialogue.

c Listen and repeat.

3 **a** Cover the dialogue. Remember with the pictures.

b Practise in fours.

4 Complete a landing card.

Surname .... Title Mr ☐ Ms ☐ Mrs ☐

First name ....

Date of birth   (day) ☐   (month) ☐   (year) ☐

Nationality ....

Address ....

.... Postcode ....

5 ° 28 ° Listen and tick ✓. Write the drinks.

Seat numbers	16E and 17E ☐	17E and 18E ☐
Flight number	BA 565 ☐	BA 654 ☐
Drinks	1 _____	2 _____
Flight to	Moscow ☐	Mexico City ☐

6 Travel phrasebook 1 *p.130*

What a wonderful world

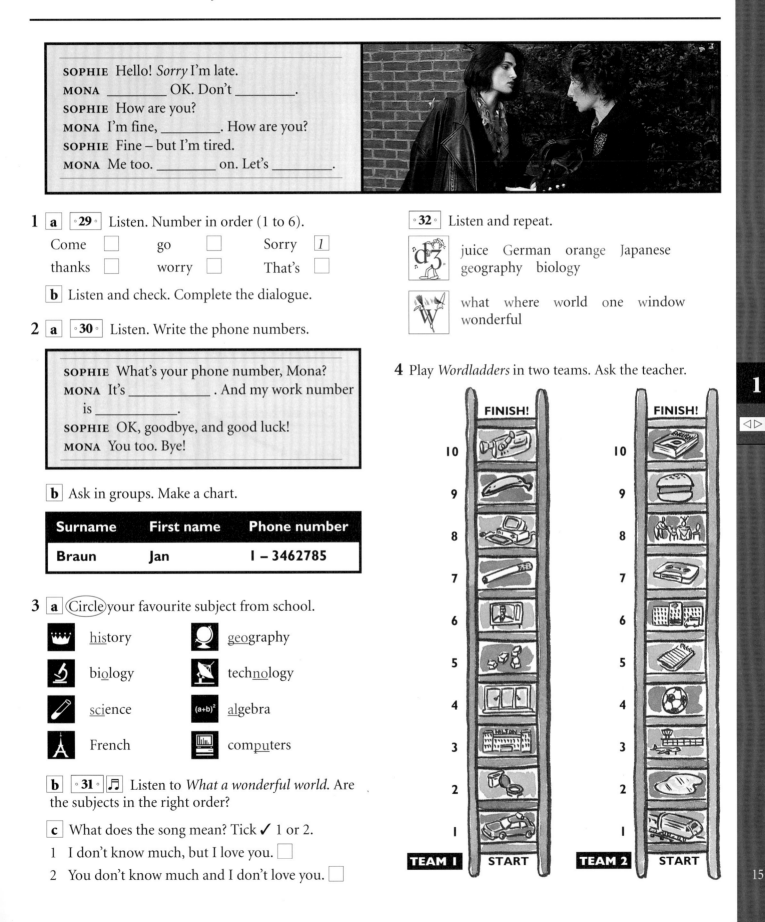

SOPHIE	Hello! *Sorry* I'm late.	
MONA	_____ OK. Don't _____.	
SOPHIE	How are you?	
MONA	I'm fine, _____. How are you?	
SOPHIE	Fine – but I'm tired.	
MONA	Me too. _____ on. Let's _____.	

1 **a** ⌜°29°⌝ Listen. Number in order (1 to 6).

Come ☐	go ☐	Sorry *1*
thanks ☐	worry ☐	That's ☐

b Listen and check. Complete the dialogue.

2 **a** ⌜°30°⌝ Listen. Write the phone numbers.

SOPHIE	What's your phone number, Mona?
MONA	It's _____ . And my work number is _____.
SOPHIE	OK, goodbye, and good luck!
MONA	You too. Bye!

b Ask in groups. Make a chart.

Surname	First name	Phone number
Braun	Jan	1 – 3462785

3 **a** (Circle) your favourite subject from school.

- history
- geography
- biology
- technology
- science
- algebra
- French
- computers

b ⌜°31°⌝ ♫ Listen to *What a wonderful world*. Are the subjects in the right order?

c What does the song mean? Tick ✓ 1 or 2.

1 I don't know much, but I love you. ☐

2 You don't know much and I don't love you. ☐

⌜°32°⌝ Listen and repeat.

juice German orange Japanese geography biology

what where world one window wonderful

4 Play *Wordladders* in two teams. Ask the teacher.

Vocabulary file 1

1 Word groups Add three words.

1 Countries *Japan* …
2 Drinks *milk* …
3 Nationalities *British* …
4 Days *Saturday* …
5 Numbers *eleven* …
6 Pronouns *he* …

2 Verbs Match the verbs and phrases.

ask listen look read ~~spell~~ write

1 *spell* a W-O-R-D
2 _____ to a cassette
3 _____ a question
4 _____ at the board
5 _____ a book
6 _____ your name

3 Questions Complete and answer.

How What When Where ~~Who~~

1 *Who*'s your teacher?
2 _____'s your name?
3 _____ are you from?
4 _____ are you?
5 _____'s your English class?

4 Prepositions Complete with in for from .

1 Coffee _____ me, please.
2 Where's Mona _____?
3 What's this _____ English?

5 English sounds Put the words in the right group.

no ~~me~~ fine student don't white please do

1   be meet seat   _me_   _____
2   you two school   _____ _____
3   go close know   _____ _____
4   ice I'm flight   _____ _____

6 Places **A** *p.133* Small objects **A** *p.134*

Study tip

■ **Make a vocabulary file.**

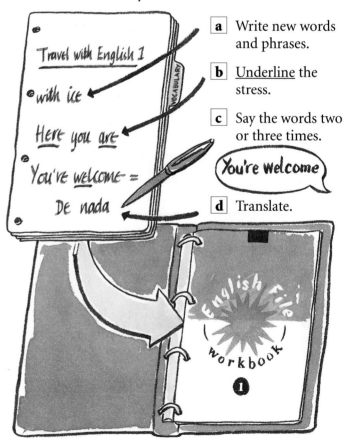

a Write new words and phrases.

b Underline the stress.

c Say the words two or three times.

d Translate.

Try it!

■ Look back at File 1. Start your vocabulary file.

Grammar file 1

1 Verb *be*: present simple

+ Positive

I	'm	
You	're	
He She It	's	German.
We You They	're	

Contractions 'm = am   's = is   're = are

☐ There are three forms: *am*, *is*, and *are*.

☐ There are eight personal pronouns: *I*,
you (singular), *he*, *she*, *it*, *we*, *you* (plural),
and *they*.

☐ *you* (s.) and *you* (pl.) are the same.

− Negative

I	'm not	
You We They	aren't	Italian.
He She It	isn't	

Contraction n't = not

☐ Use *not* after the verb to make − negatives.

? Question

Am	I	
Are	you we they	Japanese?
Is	he she it	

✓ ✗ Short answer

Yes,	I	am.	No,	I	'm not.
	you we they	are.		you we they	aren't.
	he she it	is.		he she it	isn't.

☐ Don't use contractions in + positive short answers.
Are you tired? Yes, **I am**. N O T ~~Yes, I'm.~~

Word order in questions

+			?		
Subject	**Verb**			**Verb**	**Subject**
You	're	Polish.		Are	you Polish?
She	's	from Tokyo.	Where	's	she from?

☐ Put the verb before the subject in ? questions.

2 Adjectives (1)

He's She's We're	French.

We're French.

☐ Adjectives don't change.

3 Imperatives

Verb	**+ Imperative**	**− Imperative**
open	Open the door, please!	Don't open the door.

☐ There are only two forms: positive and negative.

☐ Singular and plural imperatives are the same.

4 Possessive adjectives (1)

I	my	My name's Sophie.
you	your	What's your name?
he	his	His name's Harrison Ford.
she	her	Her name's Suzanna.

☐ Use *his* for a man and *her* for a woman.

5 Capital letters

I'm Spanish.	**P**oland	**W**ednesday	**M**ike

☐ Use CAPITAL letters for pronoun *I*, nationalities, countries,
days, and names.

▶ Workbook *p.49* Do **Grammar check 1**.

17

Lost on a train

What's this? It's an umbrella.
What are these? They're keys.

1 **a** Match the words and pictures A to J.

a watch   H
a case   ☐
a diary   ☐
a wallet   ☐
an address book ☐
an umbrella   ☐
a passport   ☐
a key   ☐
a camera   ☐
an identity card ☐

2 A
B C
D E
F G H
I
J

b Ask a partner. Point to pictures.
A What's this?
B It's a passport. What's this?

GRAMMAR FOCUS 1

Article: *a / an*

● Use *a / an* + a singular noun.

a radio	an umbrella

● Write *a* or *an*.
Use _____ + vowels (*a, e, i, o, u*).
Use _____ + consonants (*b, c, d …*).

PRACTICE

Write *a* or *an*.

1 *a* notebook   4 _____ dictionary
2 _____ hospital   5 _____ orange
3 _____ airport

2 What's in your bag / pocket?
Ask the teacher.
What's this in English?
How do you spell it?
How do you pronounce it?

3 **a** ○ 1 ○ Read and listen.

Competition

Lost on the Underground

Every year, passengers on the London
Underground lose about 120,000 objects. People
lose some very strange things, for example, a
gorilla, false teeth, a false eye, and a false leg!

These are the things people lose:

A	umbrellas	E	books	I	cameras
B	identity cards	F	diaries	J	watches
C	passports	G	cases	K	wallets
D	keys	H	bags	L	glasses

Write the top five things in the right order.

1 ☐ 2 ☐ 3 ☐ 4 ☐ 5 ☐

Send it to *The London News*, 370 Fleet Street,
London EC4 7PN.

b Close your books. Remember things A to L.

c Do the competition.

2
A

GRAMMAR FOCUS 2

Nouns

● Complete the chart.

Singular	Plural
a book	books
_____	umbrellas
a key	_____
_____	cases /ɪz/
_____	watches /ɪz/
a diary	_____

● Complete the rule.

Use *s*, _ _ , and _ _ _ to make plurals.

PRACTICE

Write the plural.

1 a chair   *chairs*   4 a country _____
2 a bus   _____   5 a bike   _____
3 a monkey _____   6 a cigarette _____

PRONUNCIATION

a ⌐ **2** ⌐

  see Spain this listen passport address

  these please isn't Brazil Thursday
Excuse me

b ⌐ **3** ⌐ Listen and repeat.

                /ɪz/

cameras   books   watches
umbrellas   passports   cases
keys   cassettes   buses
diaries   wallets   oranges

4 **a** Look at the **Competition** picture on page 18.
Ask a partner.

A What are these in English?
B They're diaries. What are these?

b Test a partner. Use all the pictures.

5 ✎ **Small objects B** *p.134*

6 Test your memory. Cover the **Competition** picture.
Remember how many.

six keys

7 **a** ⌐ **4** ⌐ Complete the numbers. Listen. <u>Underline</u>
the stress.

30	40	50
<u>thir</u>ty	_ orty	_ ifty

60	70	80
_ _ _ ty	_ _ _ _ _ ty	_ _ _ _ _ y

90	100	101
_ _ _ _ ty	a hundred	a hundred and _____

b How do you say these numbers?

31   45   57   66   74   83   99   102   189

c ►◄ *How many …?* **A** *p.118* **B** *p.121*

this = singular
these = plural

The lost property office

Are the keys on the desk?
Yes, they are.

1 **a** Match the words and pictures A to I.

the floor	*I*	the drawer	☐
the clock	☐	the shelf	☐
the cat	☐	the bin	☐
the table	☐	the wall	☐
the phone book	☐		

b Test a partner.

A What's picture D?
B The bin. What's picture H?

JOHN Put the *camera* on the _____, please, Carrie.
CARRIE Where?
JOHN Next to the _____.
CARRIE And the _____?
JOHN In the _____.
CARRIE Where are the _____?
JOHN Under the _____, next to the _____.
　Where are your glasses?

GRAMMAR FOCUS

Article: *the*

What's this in English?
It's a key.

Where's the key?

● In English, *the* doesn't change.

Singular		Plural	
the	key girl boy	the	keys girls boys

2 **a** ○ 5 ○ Listen. Circle the words you hear.

camera / cameras	drawer / drawers
shelf / shelves	case / cases
book / books	table / tables
key / keys	bag / bags

b Listen again. Complete the dialogue on page 20.

3 **a** Write *on*, *in*, *under*, or *next to*.

❶ _____ ❷ _____

❸ *on* ❹ _____

b Test a partner. **A** Close the book. **B** Ask questions about the office.
Where's the …? Where are the …?

4 **a** Where are Carrie's glasses? Read and check.

HER GLASSES ARE ON THE TABLE NEXT TO THE CHAIR UNDER THE CAT IN HER JACKET POCKET

b Play *Hide and find*. **A** 'Hide' the glasses in the picture. **B** Guess. Swap.

B Are they on the shelf next to the books?
A Yes, they are. / No, they aren't.

5 ○ 6 ○ Look at the office. Listen. Right ✓ or wrong ✗?
1 *The pens are on the desk.* ✗

this / that / these / those	
here	**there**

What's this? It's a fish.	What's that? It's a cat.
What are these? They're trees.	What are those? They're phones.

PRONUNCIATION

a ○ 7 ○

 door floor your wall water drawer

 the this these that those with

b ○ 8 ○ Listen and repeat.
'What's this?' 'It's a fish.'

6 Ask a partner about your classroom.
What's this / that? What are these / those?

7 Play *Listen and do it*. Ask the teacher.

The world of languages

> Do you speak Chinese?
> No, I don't.

1 ⚬9⚬ Listen. <u>Underline</u> the stress.

<u>A</u>rabic Chinese English German
Hindi Japanese Russian Spanish
Portuguese Italian

2 Do the quiz in pairs.

Language quiz

A **Write two languages they speak in:**

1 Canada _____

2 Algeria _____

3 Luxembourg _____

4 Taiwan _____

5 Florida, USA _____

6 Switzerland _____

☐ 12

B ⚬10⚬ **Listen. Write the six languages.**

1 _____ 4 _____

2 _____ 5 _____

3 _____ 6 _____

☐ 6

C **There are about 5,000 languages in the world. 945 are from India. What are the top three languages that people:**

speak in the world? study in Europe?

1 _____ 1 _____

2 _____ 2 _____

3 _____ 3 _____

☐ 6

Quiz score ☐ 24

3 **a** Read. Tick ✓ the right job.

teacher ☐   tourist guide ☐   translator ☐

> **Do you** speak English and two other European languages?
> **Do you** like people?
> **Do you** know much about European history?
> **Do you** want to travel round Europe with a group of Americans?
>
> **Call Gina Davis** on **0181 249 2360**.

b ⚬11⚬ Listen. Count Gina's questions.

GINA	🏴 ?	Do you speak Spanish
STEVE	✓	Yes, I do
GINA	🏴 ?	Do you speak French
STEVE	✗ 🏴 ✓	No, I don't, but I speak German
GINA	🏴 ?	Do you speak Italian
STEVE	🚬	A little
GINA	🚬 ?	Do you smoke
STEVE	✗	No, I don't
GINA	🎾 🏀 ?	Good. Do you play tennis or basketball
STEVE	🏀 ✓ 🎾 ✗	I play basketball, but I don't play tennis
GINA	🇺🇸 🍔 ?	OK. And do you like American food
STEVE	✓	Yes, I do

c Complete the dialogue with full stops (.) or question marks (?).

GINA Do you speak Spanish?

d ⚬12⚬ Listen. Repeat sentences from the dialogue.

e Cover the dialogue. Remember with the pictures.

2
C

GRAMMAR FOCUS

Present simple: *I / you / we / they*

● Complete the table.

+	−
I speak English.	I don't _____ Spanish.
?	✓ ✗
_____ you speak Italian?	Yes, I do. / No, I _____.
Contraction don't = do not	

● The verb is the same for *I*, *you*, *we*, and *they*.

PRACTICE

a Complete each sentence. Tell a partner.

1 I speak _____ very well.   ✓✓✓
2 I speak _____ quite well.   ✓✓
3 I speak a little _____.   ✓
4 I don't speak _____.   ✗

b Find two students the same as you.

A Do you speak …?
B Yes, I speak a little … / No, I don't.

4 **a** Match these words and pictures. Label the other pictures.

~~fast food~~   classical music   rock music   tennis   volleyball

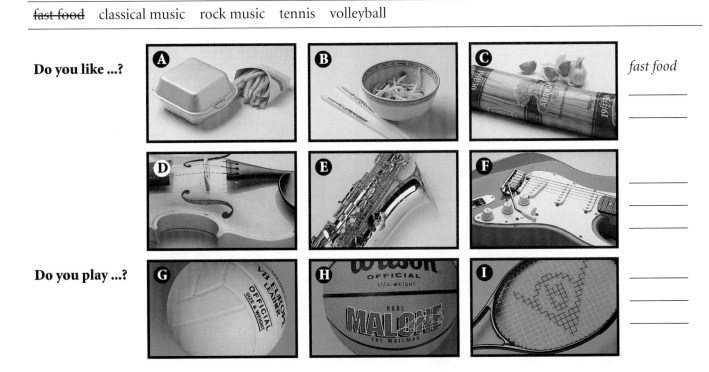

Do you like ...?

A · B · C · fast food _____ _____

D · E · F · _____ _____ _____

Do you play ...?

G · H · I · _____ _____ _____

b Ask a partner.

A Do you like (Chinese food)?
B Yes, I do. / No, I don't. / It's OK.

---

5 **a** Write six sentences with *and*, *but*, and *or*.

+		+
I like jazz	**and**	opera.

+		−
I speak English	**but**	I don't speak Italian.

−		−
I don't play tennis	**or**	volleyball.

b Give the sentences to the teacher. Play *Guess who?*

6 **a** Food and drink A *p.135*

b *Do you like …?* Ask a partner.

· 13 ·

A	but under Russian Sunday Monday London
d	do don't good doctor study India

Low salary? High stress?

> *What do you do?*
> *I'm a photographer.*

1 📖 Time A *p.136*

2 **a** Number in the right order (1st to 6th).

Yes, I do.	☐
No, I'm not. I'm your new manager.	☐
I'm a journalist. Are you my new secretary?	☐
Do you work here?	*1st*
Oh!	☐
What do you do?	☐

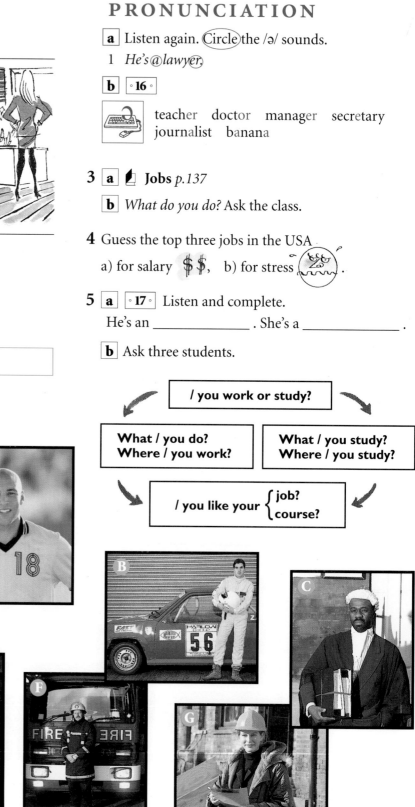

b ◦ **14** ◦ Listen and check. Practise.

GRAMMAR FOCUS

● Use *a / an* + jobs.

I'm **a** teacher. NOT ~~I'm teacher.~~

PRACTICE

a Match the sentences and pictures.

1	*He's a <u>law</u>yer.*	*C*
2	_____ <u>pi</u>lot.	☐
3	_____ <u>fire</u>fighter.	☐
4	_____ <u>ra</u>cing <u>dri</u>ver.	☐
5	_____ <u>doc</u>tor.	☐
6	_____ <u>foot</u>baller.	☐
7	_____ engi<u>neer</u>.	☐

b ◦ **15** ◦ Complete with *He's / She's* and *a / an*. Listen and check.

PRONUNCIATION

a Listen again. ⃝Circle⃝ the /ə/ sounds.

1 *He's ⃝a⃝ law⃝yer⃝.*

b ◦ **16** ◦

teacher   doc⃝tor⃝   manager   secretary   journalist   banana

3 **a** 📖 Jobs *p.137*

b *What do you do?* Ask the class.

4 Guess the top three jobs in the USA
a) for salary $ $,   b) for stress ⃝😖⃝ .

5 **a** ◦ **17** ◦ Listen and complete.
He's an _____ . She's a _____ .

b Ask three students.

/ you work or study?

What / you do? **Where / you work?**	**What / you study?** **Where / you study?**

/ you like your { job? course? }

2

D

How much is that?

1 **a** °18° Listen and tick ✓.

1 How much does she change?

$50 ☐ $100 ☐ $150 ☐

2 How much does she get?

£25 ☐   £75 ☐   £100 ☐

b Listen again. Number in order (1 to 6).

Today's exchange rates
£1 = 2 dollars / 1.6 euros

Do you have a pen?	☐
Here you are.	☐
Can I see your passport?	☐
Just a moment.	☐
Can I change $…, please?	1
Sign here, please.	☐

c Listen and repeat.

d Practise in pairs with **Today's exchange rates**.

£1.00 = one pound   **v**
£2.50 = two pounds fifty
45p = forty-five pence (or 'p')

2 **a** °19° Listen. What does he have? How much is it?

Orange juice / Apple juice	regular	95p	large	£1.70
Tea / Coffee		95p		
Coke	regular	80p	large	£1.50
Pizza	regular	£4.00	large	£5.00
Cheeseburger		£3.25		
Steak sandwich		£5.50		
Tuna sandwich		£2.75		
Chips		£1.50		
Salad		£1.50		

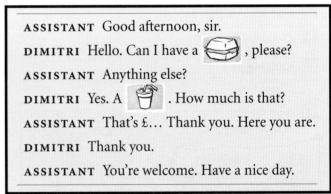

b Listen again. Remember the dialogue.

ASSISTANT Good afternoon, sir.

DIMITRI Hello. Can I have a 🍔 , please?

ASSISTANT Anything else?

DIMITRI Yes. A 🥤 . How much is that?

ASSISTANT That's £… Thank you. Here you are.

DIMITRI Thank you.

ASSISTANT You're welcome. Have a nice day.

c Role-play. **A** You're the assistant. **B** and **C** You're customers.

3 **a** °20° Listen and repeat.

thir<u>teen</u> <u>thir</u>ty four<u>teen</u> <u>for</u>ty · fif<u>teen</u> <u>fif</u>ty
six<u>teen</u> <u>six</u>ty seven<u>teen</u> <u>se</u>venty
eigh<u>teen</u> <u>eigh</u>ty nine<u>teen</u> <u>nine</u>ty

b °21° Listen. Circle the right price.

1 £17 / £70   3 £14 / £40

2 £19 / £90   4 £5.18 / £5.80

4 🧳 Travel phrasebook 2 *p.130*

Why do you want to learn English?

1 Complete the form.

English File survey

Are you married?

How old are you?

I'm thirty-five.

1	Surname
2	First name
3	Nationality
4	Town / City
5	Address
6	Phone no.
7	Marital status: single ☐ married ☐
8	Age
9	Occupation
10	Languages

11 Why do you want to learn English?

Number your top three (1st, 2nd, 3rd).

for my job ☐   to study ☐

to travel ☐   to meet people ☐

to translate ☐

to understand songs / films ☐

other (what?) _____ ☐

12 Tick ✓. Do you need to …?

listen ☐   speak ☐   read ☐   write ☐

2 **a** Write questions for 1 to 10.

  1 *What's your surname?*

b ○22○ Listen and check. Repeat the questions.

3 Interview a partner. Compare answers.

4 **a** ○23○ Listen. Number the pictures in the right order.

tired ☐   cold ☐1☐   happy ☐

hungry ☐   thirsty ☐   hot ☐

(not) very / quite		
I'm	(not) very / quite	tired.

b Ask a partner.

  A Are you (tired)?

  B Yes, I am. I'm (quite tired). / No, I'm not. I'm not (very tired).

5 **a** ○24○ Listen. Write the questions in the right column.

Do you …?	**Are you …?** *tired*

b Ask a partner questions. What do you have in common?

6 Write four sentences.

  We speak … We don't like … We're …

○25○

first   third   work   learn   verb   surname

2

Vocabulary file 2

1 Word groups Add words for two minutes.

1 Small objects *identity card* …
2 Languages *Hungarian* …
3 Food *orange* …
4 Ordinals *second* …
5 Jobs *politician* …

2 Verbs Match the verbs and phrases.

> answer ~~like~~ put play say speak study

1 *like* Chinese food
2 _____ your pen on the table
3 _____ 'Good morning'
4 _____ a question
5 _____ biology
6 _____ volleyball
7 _____ English

3 Stress Count the syllables. Mark the stress.

Word stress

Eng | lish = two syllables

English
ENGlish = stress on the first syllable
▬ ▬
Eng lish

1 Arabic ☐   5 Brazil ☐
2 Japanese ☐   6 American ☐
3 language ☐   7 welcome ☐
4 Italian ☐

4 Grammar words (Circle) the different word.

1 Verbs: smoke know listen (window)
2 Singular nouns: radio students case desk
3 Plural nouns: class drawers diaries buses
4 Articles: a be an the
5 Adjectives: French thirsty hot Italy
6 Possessive adjectives: my he your her

5 Prepositions Complete with in next to on under.

1 The police officer's _____ the car.
2 The dog's _____ the car.
3 The man's _____ the car.
4 The woman's _____ the car.

6 English sounds Match the pictures and groups 1 to 4.

☐ 3   ☐   ☐   ☐

1 day make paper plane station
2 again water doctor hospital American
3 give little English married syllable
4 door four morning or all

7 🔊 **Numbers B** *p.132* 🔊 **House A** *p.138*

Study tip
··
■ Use a bi-lingual dictionary.

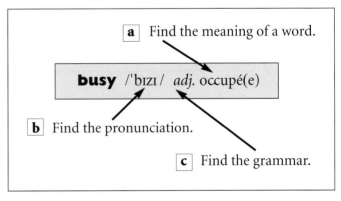

a Find the meaning of a word.

busy /ˈbɪzɪ/ *adj.* occupé(e)

b Find the pronunciation.

c Find the grammar.

Try it!

■ Find these words in your dictionary.

> angry break ghost kill stairs

■ Find two words you want to learn: one for your job and one to travel.
··

Grammar file 2

1 Articles

☐ There are only two articles in English: *a* / *an* and *the*.

a / *an* (indefinite article)

It's	a	cassette. bag.
	an	office. umbrella.

It's a bus.

☐ Use *a* / *an* + a singular noun.
☐ Use *an* + vowels (*a, e, i, o, u*).
☐ Use *a* / *an* + jobs. I'm **a** doctor. NOT ~~I'm doctor.~~

the (definite article)

It's the bus to the airport.

Open	the /ðə/	door / windows.
	the /ðiː/	envelope / umbrellas.

☐ Use *the* + singular and plural nouns.
☐ Say /ðiː/ for *the* + vowels.

2 Nouns

Singular	Plural	Spelling
a book an engineer	books engineers	+ s

Also

a watch a fax	watches /ɪz/ faxes	+ es (after -ch, -sh, -s, -x, -z)
a country a city	countries cities	consonant + y → ies

☐ Use -s, -es, and -ies to make plurals.
☐ Don't use *a* / *an* + plural nouns.
They're **books**. NOT ~~They're a books.~~

3 *How much …? / How many …?*

'How many sandwiches?' 'Four, please.'
'How much is that?' 'It's twelve dollars.'

☐ Use *How many …?* + plural nouns.
☐ Use *How much …?* + money.

4 *this / that / these / those*

☐ Use *this* / *that* + a singular noun.
☐ Use *these* / *those* + plural nouns.

5 Present simple: *I / you / we / they*

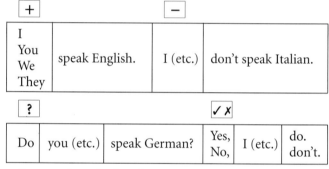

+		–	
I You We They	speak English.	I (etc.)	don't speak Italian.

?			✓✗		
Do	you (etc.)	speak German?	Yes, No,	I (etc.)	do. don't.

Contraction don't = do not

☐ The verb is the same for *I*, *you*, *we*, and *they*.
☐ Use *do* / *don't* (= the auxiliary) in short answers.
Do you like tea? Yes, I **do**. NOT ~~Yes, I like.~~

6 Adjectives (2)

I'm / You're (etc.)	quite (not) very	tired.

☐ *quite* and (*not*) *very* go before the adjective.

7 Age

'How old are you?' 'I'm twenty-nine (years old).'

☐ Use verb *be* + age. NOT ~~I have twenty-nine.~~

▶ Workbook *p.50* Do **Grammar check 2**. ▶ **Progress chart** (Files 1 / 2) *p.2*. ▶ Do **Check your progress** *p.29*.

Check your progress

Grammar   Right ✓ = **1** point

1 Write the questions.

Egyptian you are? *Are you Egyptian?*
1 are where from you?
2 you speak do Italian?
3 American is Michael Caine?
4 work do where they?
5 spell do how you it?   ☐ 5

2 Write the negatives.

I'm German. *I'm not German.*
1 We're Turkish.
2 It's a Japanese video.
3 They speak Portuguese.
4 Write your name!
5 Linda's Polish.   ☐ 5

3 Complete the dialogues.

Is he Argentinian? Yes, he *is.*
1 _____ Carla Spanish? No, she _____.
2 _____ BMW cars German? Yes, they _____.
3 _____ you English? Yes, I _____.
4 _____ you speak Chinese? No, I _____.
5 _____ you like jazz? Yes, I _____.   ☐ 5

4 Write the contractions.

She is hungry. *She's hungry.*
1 He is not Greek.
2 We are Swedish.
3 I am not thirsty.
4 They do not like rock music.
5 What is your phone number?   ☐ 5

5 Write *and, but,* or *or*.

We like coffee *but* we don't like tea.
1 I play basketball _____ golf.
2 They don't speak French _____ Arabic.
3 I like chocolate _____ bananas _____
   I don't like apples _____ oranges.   ☐ 5

6 Write *a, an, the,* or – .

I work in *a* bank in Bucharest.
1 She's _____ doctor.
2 They live in _____ Mexico.
3 Open _____ door, please.
4 What's this? It's _____ identity card.
5 Here is the taxi to _____ station.   ☐ 5

7 Write the plurals.

I'm a doctor. *We're doctors.*
1 It's a dictionary.
2 She's a nurse.
3 This is a Japanese watch.
4 That's my key.
5 You're French.   ☐ 5

Total ☐ 35

Fluency

1 In English, can you …?   Yes ✓

count from 20 to 1 / from 1st to 10th. ☐
say your phone number. ☐
spell your first name and surname. ☐
say the days of the week. ☐
ask a partner five questions. ☐

2 What do you say?

Buy a 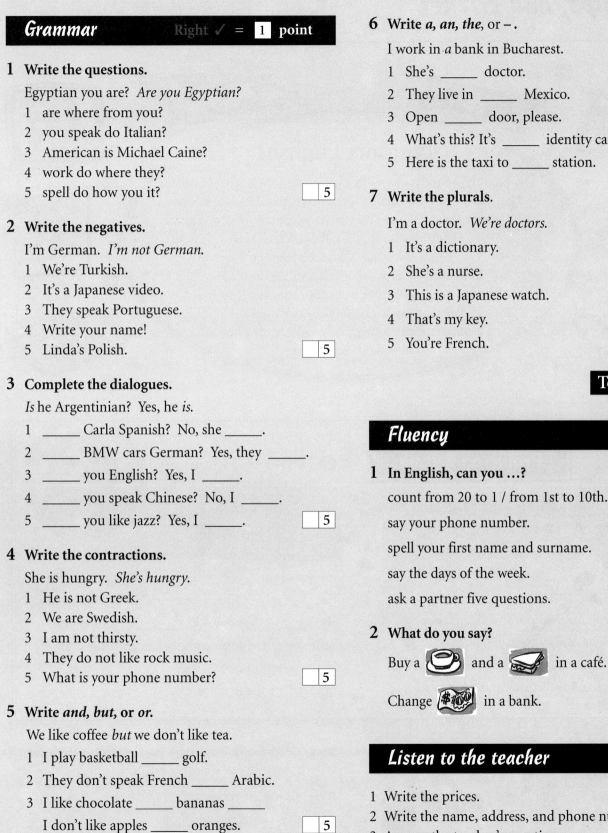 and a ▨ in a café.

Change 💵 in a bank.

Listen to the teacher

1 Write the prices.
2 Write the name, address, and phone number.
3 Answer the teacher's questions.

Fish, chips, and cricket

*Does he live in a house?
No, he doesn't.*

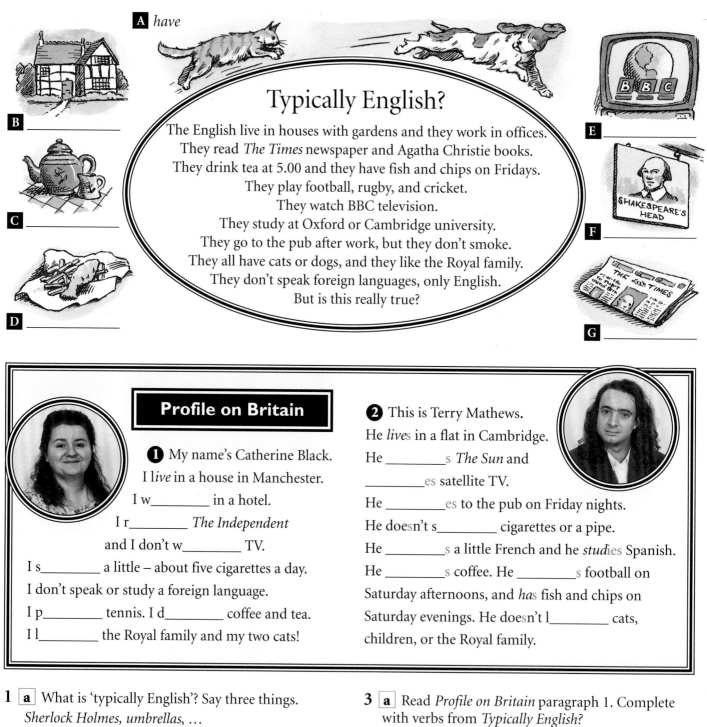

A *have*

B _____

C _____

D _____

E _____

F _____

G _____

Typically English?

The English live in houses with gardens and they work in offices.
They read *The Times* newspaper and Agatha Christie books.
They drink tea at 5.00 and they have fish and chips on Fridays.
They play football, rugby, and cricket.
They watch BBC television.
They study at Oxford or Cambridge university.
They go to the pub after work, but they don't smoke.
They all have cats or dogs, and they like the Royal family.
They don't speak foreign languages, only English.
But is this really true?

3

A

Profile on Britain

❶ My name's Catherine Black.
I *live* in a house in Manchester.
I w_____ in a hotel.
I r_____ *The Independent*
and I don't w_____ TV.
I s_____ a little – about five cigarettes a day.
I don't speak or study a foreign language.
I p_____ tennis. I d_____ coffee and tea.
I l_____ the Royal family and my two cats!

❷ This is Terry Mathews.
He *lives* in a flat in Cambridge.
He _____s *The Sun* and
_____es satellite TV.
He _____es to the pub on Friday nights.
He doesn't s_____ cigarettes or a pipe.
He _____s a little French and he *studies* Spanish.
He _____s coffee. He _____s football on
Saturday afternoons, and *has* fish and chips on
Saturday evenings. He doesn't l_____ cats,
children, or the Royal family.

1 **a** What is 'typically English'? Say three things.
Sherlock Holmes, umbrellas, …

b ○ **1** ○ Read *Typically English?* Are your three things in the text?

c Find verbs / phrases for pictures A to G.

2 Dictation. *The English today*. Write the statistics.
30% smoke.

3 **a** Read *Profile on Britain* paragraph 1. Complete with verbs from *Typically English?*

b Complete paragraph 2.

c ○ **2** ○ Listen and check.

GRAMMAR FOCUS

Present simple: *he / she / it*

● Look at the verbs in paragraphs 1 and 2. What's the difference?

● Write one letter.

> ⊞ Present simple verbs with *he* and *she* (and *it*) end in ___.

> **Contraction**   doesn't = does not

PRACTICE

a Complete the sentences.

1 They read *The Times*.
  She *reads The Independent.*

2 I don't like cats.
  He _____ like cats.

3 Do they drink coffee?
  _____ she drink coffee? Yes, she _____ .

4 Do you live in Paris?
  _____ he live in Paris? No, he _____ .

b Find the *he / she / it* form of these verbs.

watch *watches* /ɪz/	have _____
study _____	do _____ /dʌz/
play _____	go _____ /gəʊz/

4 **a** Tick ✓ or cross ✗ the chart.

	Catherine	Terry
🚬	✓	
📺		
🐱		
⚽		

b Ask a partner with the chart.

A Does (Catherine smoke)?
B Yes, she does. / No, she doesn't. Does …?

PRONUNCIATION

⚬ 3 ⚬ Listen and repeat.

1 Does <u>Catherine</u> <u>live</u> in <u>Man</u>chester? <u>Yes</u>, she <u>does</u>.
2 Does she <u>watch</u> <u>TV</u>? <u>No</u>, she <u>does</u>n't. She <u>does</u>n't <u>watch</u> <u>TV</u>.
3 Does he <u>smoke</u>? <u>No</u>, he <u>does</u>n't. He <u>does</u>n't <u>smoke</u>.

5 **a** Write questions 7 and 8. Interview the teacher. Tick ✓ (= Yes, I do.) or cross ✗ (= No, I don't.).
Do you smoke?

		Teacher	Partner
1	🚬		
2	live in a 🏠		
3	read a 📰		
4	play ⚽		
5	drink ☕		
6	listen to 🎵		
7			
8			

b Interview a partner. ✓ or ✗ the answers.

c Swap partners. Ask about your first partners.
Does he / she smoke?

6 **a** **⚬ 4 ⚬** Listen. What nationality is he?

b Write five sentences about a 'typical man' or 'typical woman' from your country.

⚬ 5 ⚬

	man flat have thanks married classical
🌼	live five very video evening television

Through the keyhole

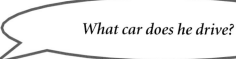

What car does he drive?

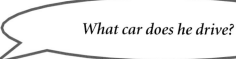

Mystery man	**?**	**Who's our mystery man this week ?** **Look at the ten clues.**

(not) eat meat *E*   drive an Aston Martin ☐   like fishing ☐   play the cello ☐   paint pictures ☐

have two children ☐   speak French and German ☐   ride a horse ☐   live in London ☐   write books ☐

1 **a** Match the phrases and pictures A to J.

b Make sentences.
He doesn't eat meat.

2 Write the verbs. Answer the questions.

1 What car does he *drive*?
He drives an Aston Martin.

2 How many children does he _____ ?

3 Where does he _____ ?

4 What languages does he _____ ?

5 Does he _____ a bike?

6 Does he _____ the piano?

PRONUNCIATION

° 6 ° Listen to exercise 2. Repeat.

1 <u>What car</u> does he <u>drive</u>? He <u>drives</u> an <u>Aston Martin.</u>

3 **a** Close your books. What can you remember?
He lives in London.

b **° 7 °** Guess. Who is he? What does he do?
Listen and check.

GRAMMAR FOCUS

Present simple: questions

● Questions with *be* swap subject and verb.

> She's a secretary.
>
> **Is she** a secretary?

● Other verbs need help! Add *Do / Does*.

> They live in a flat.   **Do** they live in a flat?
> He work in a bank.   **Does** he work in a bank?

● Question word before *do / does*.

Question	Auxiliary	Subject	Infinitive
	Do	you	smoke?
Where	does	she	live?
What	do	they	do?
What languages	does	John	speak?

4 **a** Write questions.
Where do you live?

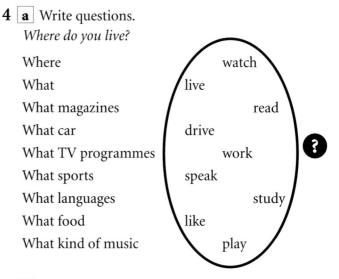

Where
What
What magazines
What car
What TV programmes
What sports
What languages
What food
What kind of music

watch
live
read
drive
work
speak
study
like
play

?

b In fours, ask questions for two minutes. How many things do you all have in common?

5 Play *Through the keyhole*. Choose a mystery person. Write six clues.

° 8 °

they're   there   where   compare
Hungarian   airport

food   phrase   fifty   photo   coffee
different

can / can't Verbs: *sing* / *dance*, etc.

What can you do?

Can you dance?
No, I can't.

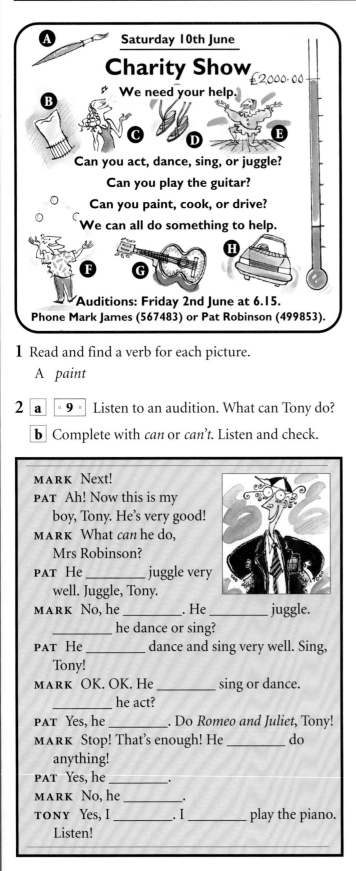

A Saturday 10th June

Charity Show £2,000.00

B We need your help.

C **D** **E**

Can you act, dance, sing, or juggle?

Can you play the guitar?

Can you paint, cook, or drive?

We can all do something to help.

F **G** **H**

Auditions: Friday 2nd June at 6.15.
Phone Mark James (567483) or Pat Robinson (499853).

1 Read and find a verb for each picture.

A *paint*

2 **a** ° 9 ° Listen to an audition. What can Tony do?

b Complete with *can* or *can't*. Listen and check.

MARK Next!
PAT Ah! Now this is my
boy, Tony. He's very good!
MARK What *can* he do,
Mrs Robinson?
PAT He _____ juggle very
well. Juggle, Tony.
MARK No, he _____. He _____ juggle.
_____ he dance or sing?
PAT He _____ dance and sing very well. Sing,
Tony!
MARK OK. OK. He _____ sing or dance.
_____ he act?
PAT Yes, he _____. Do *Romeo and Juliet*, Tony!
MARK Stop! That's enough! He _____ do
anything!
PAT Yes, he _____.
MARK No, he _____.
TONY Yes, I _____. I _____ play the piano.
Listen!

GRAMMAR FOCUS

can / can't

● Complete the chart with *can* or *can't* + infinitive.

+	He _____.	Здравствуйте!
−	She _____.	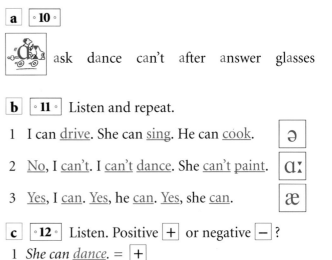
?	_____ you _____?	
✓✗	Yes, I _____. / No, I _____.	
Contraction	can't = cannot	

PRACTICE

What can you do for the show? Point and ask with pictures A to H.

A Can you juggle?
B Yes, I can. / No, I can't. Can you …?

PRONUNCIATION

a ° 10 °

ask dance can't after answer glasses

b ° 11 ° Listen and repeat.

1 I can <u>drive</u>. She can <u>sing</u>. He can <u>cook</u>. ə

2 <u>No</u>, I <u>can't</u>. I <u>can't</u> <u>dance</u>. She <u>can't</u> <u>paint</u>. ɑː

3 <u>Yes</u>, I <u>can</u>. <u>Yes</u>, he <u>can</u>. <u>Yes</u>, she <u>can</u>. æ

c 12 Listen. Positive **+** or negative **−** ?
1 *She can <u>dance</u>.* = **+**

3 **a** ✎ Verbs A *p.139*

b *Can you …?* Ask the class. Find a different
student for each verb.

4 Write three true sentences with *can* / *can't*.

3

C

34

It's + time   The time, *second* / *minute*, etc.

Race the clock

> **What's the time in Tokyo?**
> **It's three o'clock in the afternoon.**

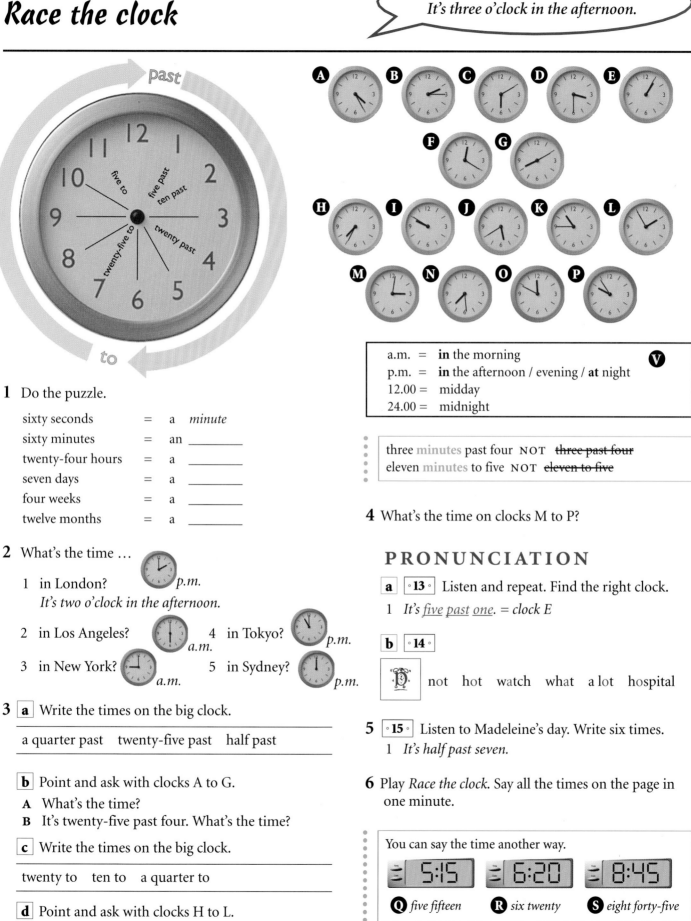

past

to

1 Do the puzzle.

sixty seconds	=	a	*minute*
sixty minutes	=	an	_____
twenty-four hours	=	a	_____
seven days	=	a	_____
four weeks	=	a	_____
twelve months	=	a	_____

2 What's the time …

1 in London?   *p.m.*
   It's two o'clock in the afternoon.

2 in Los Angeles?   4 in Tokyo? *p.m.*
   a.m.

3 in New York?   5 in Sydney?
   a.m.   *p.m.*

3 **a** Write the times on the big clock.

a quarter past   twenty-five past   half past

b Point and ask with clocks A to G.
   A What's the time?
   B It's twenty-five past four. What's the time?

c Write the times on the big clock.

twenty to   ten to   a quarter to

d Point and ask with clocks H to L.

---

a.m. =	**in** the morning
p.m. =	**in** the afternoon / evening / **at** night
12.00 =	midday
24.00 =	midnight

V

three **minutes** past four NOT ~~three past four~~
eleven **minutes** to five NOT ~~eleven to five~~

4 What's the time on clocks M to P?

PRONUNCIATION

a ◦**13**◦ Listen and repeat. Find the right clock.
1 *It's five past one.* = *clock E*

b ◦**14**◦

not   hot   watch   what   a lot   hospital

5 ◦**15**◦ Listen to Madeleine's day. Write six times.
1 *It's half past seven.*

6 Play *Race the clock*. Say all the times on the page in one minute.

You can say the time another way.

5:15   **6:20**   **8:45**

Q *five fifteen*   **R** *six twenty*   **S** *eight forty-five*

At the hotel

TRAVEL WITH ENGLISH

ISABEL Good afternoon. Do y_____ h_____ any rooms, please?

RECEPTIONIST Yes. Would you like a double room, madam?

ISABEL No, tw_____ s_____ r_____, p_____ .

RECEPTIONIST With or without bathrooms?

ISABEL W_____.

RECEPTIONIST Fine. How many nights would you like to stay?

ISABEL Just one. H_____ m_____ i_____ it a night?

RECEPTIONIST $80 each, including breakfast. Can I see your passports, please?

ISABEL H_____ y_____ a_____.

RECEPTIONIST Thank you. Rooms 207 and 208 on the second floor. Here are your keys.

ISABEL T_____. Where's the lift?

RECEPTIONIST It's over there.

1 Match the words and pictures A to F.

single room	C	double room	☐
bath	☐	shower	☐
on the first floor	☐	lift	☐

2 **a** Read the dialogue. Imagine what Isabel says.

b ° 16 ° Listen and check. Complete the dialogue.

c Practise in pairs.

3 **a** ° 17 ° Listen and answer.

1 How much are the rooms?
2 Does he make a reservation?

b Listen again. Complete the form.

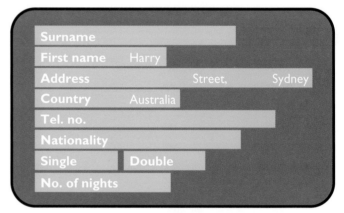

Surname	
First name	Harry
Address	Street, Sydney
Country	Australia
Tel. no.	
Nationality	
Single	**Double**
No. of nights	

4 ° 18 ° Check into a hotel. You don't have a reservation. Listen and answer.

5 **a** **Role-play 1.** **A** You're the receptionist. **B** Phone and make a reservation.

b **Role-play 2.** Swap. **A** Arrive and check in. **B** You're the receptionist.

6 🛅 **Travel phrasebook 3** *p.130*

The Edinburgh Festival

The Edinburgh Festival is the largest arts festival in the world. It starts on the second Sunday in August and finishes three weeks later.

INTERCITY	London – Edinburgh
King's Cross	**Edinburgh**
Depart	*Arrive*
06.00	10.50
08.00	13.30
10.00	15.25

Festival Guide: . August 9th

Theatre: *Waiting for Godot* by Samuel Beckett
The Festival Club
3.45 p.m. – 5.00 p.m., £6.50

Music: John Renbourn in Concert
Acoustic Music Centre
____ a.m. – 12.00 p.m., £6.00

Cinema: *La Dolce Vita* (Fellini)
Film House
8.00 p.m. – ____ p.m., £5.50

Cafés and bars	
Assembly Café:	open 10.00 a.m. – ____ p.m. for breakfast and lunch
Pleasance Jazz Club:	open ____ p.m. – 3.00 a.m.
Main Theatre Bar:	open ____ p.m. – 4.00 a.m.

Edinburgh Castle
Open April – September every day 9.30 a.m. – 6.00 p.m.

Opening and closing times in Scotland		
	Open	**Close**
Banks	09.15	4.45
Post offices	09.00	____ (Monday – Friday)
		13.00 (Saturdays)
Shops	09.00	____ or ____

1 Read and answer.

1 What time does the first train leave London?
It *leaves at six o'clock.*

2 What time does it arrive in Edinburgh?
It *arrives* _____

3 What time does the castle open?
It _____

4 What time does it close?
_____

5 What time does *Waiting for Godot* start?
_____

6 What time does it finish?
_____

7 What time do the banks open?
They *open* _____

8 What time do they close?
They _____

● The present simple for *it* is the same as for *he* and *she*.

What time does the castle open? It opens at 9.30.

PRONUNCIATION

19 Listen to exercise 1. Repeat.

1 *What time does the first train leave London?*

2 Ask the teacher. Complete the information.
What time does John Renbourn in Concert start?

3 **20** Listen. Complete the chart.

What?	What time?	How much?
Military Tattoo	7.45 and ___ p.m.	£7.50 – £ ___
Death in Venice	___ p.m.	£ ___
I'm not a feminist but …	___ p.m.	£ ___
_____ music	___ p.m.	£ ___

4 ►◄ **Day trip A** *p.119* **B** *p.122*

5 Write information about your town for tourists.
In Bilbao, the banks open at 8.00 in the morning and close at 2.00 in the afternoon.

Vocabulary file 3

1 Puzzle Write the missing word.

1 England / English   Germany / *German*
2 this / these   that / _____
3 one / first   two / _____
4 a car / cars   a bus / _____
5 leave / arrive   stop / _____
6 I / my   he / _____

2 Verbs Match the verbs and phrases.

drive go ~~have~~ live play ride watch work

1 *have* a cat and a dog
2 _____ in an office
3 _____ a horse
4 _____ the piano
5 _____ TV
6 _____ a car
7 _____ to a café
8 _____ in a flat

3 Questions Complete and answer.

How many How much ~~How~~ What time What

1 *How* do you pronounce 'cassette'?
2 _____ cigarettes do you smoke a day?
3 _____ is a single room?
4 _____ newspaper do you read?
5 _____ do the banks open?

4 Grammar words Label the sentences.

~~question word~~ noun subject article auxiliary
question mark verb (infinitive) preposition

a *question word*   c _____
    b _____   d _____

    Where does she work? In a factory.

e _____   f _____

        g _____   h _____

5 Prepositions Complete with of to with without .

1 He goes _____ the pub on Friday nights.
2 Can I have a piece _____ paper, please?
3 'Black coffee' is coffee _____ milk.
4 Can I have a room _____ a bathroom, please?

6 English sounds ⟨Circle⟩ the different word.

1 desk ten Let's ⟨need⟩ twelve very
2 flat language man name thanks travel
3 garden glasses case half past large
4 hot phone sorry stop watch want

7 ✎ Verbs B *p.139*

Study tip

■ Test yourself regularly.

[a] Test yourself or a partner.

[b] Look at new words after the class / the next day and before the next class / after a week, etc.

Try it!

■ ✎ **Time B** *p.136* Learn the months and seasons.

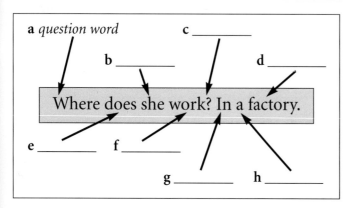

3
V

Grammar file 3

1 Present simple: *he / she / it*

+

I You We They	speak English.
He She It	speak**s** English.

Don't forget the 'S' for he/she/it

☐ There are only two forms: *speak* and *speaks*.
☐ Infinitive (= verb) + *s* for *he*, *she*, and *it*.
  NOT ~~She speak … / She's speaks …~~

−

I (etc.)	don't	speak English.
He She It	doesn't	speak English.

?   ✓✗

Do	I (etc.)	speak English?	Yes, No,	I (etc.)	do. don't.
Does	he she it	speak English?	Yes, No,	he she it	does. doesn't.

Contraction doesn't = does not

☐ Use *does / doesn't* + infinitive in **−** and **?** .
  NOT ~~He doesn't smokes. / Does it starts at 3.00?~~

Infinitive	Present simple	Spelling
read	She reads *Newsweek*.	+ s
finish	The film finishes /ɪz/ at 10 p.m.	+ es (after -ch, -sh, -s, -x, -z)
study	He studies biology.	consonant + y → ies

☐ Spelling rules are the same as nouns. ▶ **Nouns** *p.28*
☐ Remember: *have* → *has*, *go* → *goes* /gəʊz/, *do* → *does* /dʌz/.

Word order in questions

Question	**A**uxiliary	**S**ubject	**I**nfinitive	
	Do Does	you she	live play	here? tennis?
Where What What time	do does does	they John the bank	work? study? open?	

☐ Remember: word order = **A** **S** **I** and **Q** **A** **S** **I** .

2 *can / can't*

+   **−**

I / You / We / They He / She / It	can swim.	I (etc.)	can't swim.

?   ✓✗

Can	I (etc.)	drive?	Yes, No,	I (etc.)	can. can't.

Contraction can't = cannot

☐ Use *can* + infinitive. NOT ~~I can to swim~~.
☐ *can* is the same for all pronouns (*I / he*, etc.).
☐ *can* has two meanings:

Can you close the window, please?   *I can ski*

3 The time

What's the time? It's	eight o'clock. half past three.

☐ Use *It's* + time.
✎ **Time** *p.136*

4 Prepositions of time (1)

It opens	in	the morning / afternoon / evening.
	on	Saturday (morning).
	at	six o'clock.

☐ Use *in* for parts of the day, *on* for days, and *at* for times.
☐ Remember: **at** night.

▶ Workbook *p.51* Do **Grammar check 3**.

(*not*) *very* / *quite* + adjectives   Adjectives: *old* / *blue*, etc.

What's red, fast, and Italian?

> *Is he tall?*
> *No, he's quite short.*

1 **a** (Circle) the adjectives.
(Nice) to meet you   We're tired   Good evening
Chinese food   Happy New Year

b What other adjectives do you know?

2 **a** Number the colours 1 to 11.

yellow — 11
blue
green
grey
pink
purple
red
orange
white
black
brown

b ⌐1⌐ Listen and check.

c Test a partner with pictures 1 to 11.
A What colour is it / are they?
B It's / They're (yellow). What colour …

3 Write the colours.

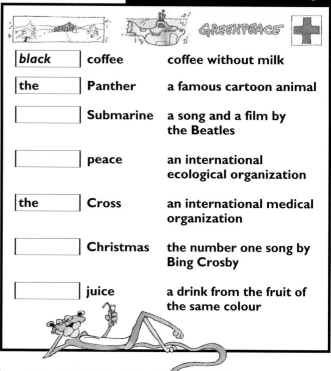

COLOURFUL NAMES

black	coffee	coffee without milk
the	Panther	a famous cartoon animal
	Submarine	a song and a film by the Beatles
	peace	an international ecological organization
the	Cross	an international medical organization
	Christmas	the number one song by Bing Crosby
	juice	a drink from the fruit of the same colour

GRAMMAR FOCUS

Adjectives

● Look at exercises 1 to 3. (Circle) the right rule.
Adjectives **change** / **don't change** in singular and plural.

Adjectives usually go **before** / **after** the noun.

PRACTICE

Write sentences.

1 a house / old *It's an old house.*
2 shoes / new
  They're _____
3 a watch / expensive
  _____
4 girls / Hungarian
  _____
5 a car / fast
  _____
6 jeans / cheap
  _____

40

4 **a** ✎ Adjectives A *p.140*

b Write three sentences for each picture A to G.
F *It's Japanese. It's new. It isn't cheap.*

5 **a** ✎ Adjectives B *p.140* Think of a famous person for each adjective.

b Describe these people. Use *very*, *quite*, and *not very*.
M *He's very tall. He's quite good-looking.*

6 **a** Write about somebody for the class to guess.

He's American. He's from Brooklyn in the USA. He's about forty. He's very tall and quite thin. He's quite good-looking. He's a famous actor and a very funny comedian. He sings and directs films, too.
He's the Beverly Hills Cop. His first name is E_____ and his surname is M_____.

b Play *Who is it?* **A** Think of a famous person.
B, **C**, **D** Guess who it is in ten questions.

∘ 2 ∘

  yes you your young year yellow

  do two June blue food juice

/juː/ use new music student university

A royal ghost story

Who's your mother's father's daughter?

H·A·M·L·E·T

by
WILLIAM
SHAKESPEARE

To be or not to be...

The King of Denmark, old Hamlet, is married to Queen Gertrude. The King's brother, Claudius, wants to be king. He kills old Hamlet and gets married to Gertrude. The King's son, young Hamlet, comes home from university. His father's ghost tells Hamlet to kill his uncle Claudius …

YOUNG HAMLET ....the Prince of Denmark, Claudius's *nephew*
OLD KING HAMLET .... Hamlet's *father*
CLAUDIUS.............................. the old King's *brother*, Gertrude's second *husband*
GERTRUDE...Claudius's *wife*, Hamlet's *mother*
OPHELIA .... Hamlet's *girlfriend*, Polonius's *daughter*
LAERTES .... Ophelia's *brother*, Polonius's *son*
POLONIUS.............................. Laertes and Ophelia's *father*, Claudius's *friend*
HORATIO...Hamlet's *friend*

Gertrude   Old Hamlet (1st, dead)   Claudius (2nd)   Polonius

Horatio   Young Hamlet   Ophelia   Laertes

1 **a** ⟨ 3 ⟩ Listen. <u>Underline</u> the stress on the names.

b Complete the chart.

👨	👩	**Plural**
grandfather	grandmother	(grandparents)
father	*mother*	(parents)
husband	_____	
son	_____	(children)
_____	sister	
_____	aunt	
cousin	cousin	
boyfriend	_____	
_____	friend	
nephew	niece	

⟨ 4 ⟩

👶   the   father   brother   grandmother
grandfather

⬆️   son   husband   cousin   brother   mother

GRAMMAR FOCUS

Possessive *'s*

Gertrude is Hamlet's mother.
McDonald's restaurant
Beethoven's fifth symphony

● Use *'s* not *the ... of ...* NOT ~~the mother of Hamlet~~

PRACTICE

Write sentences.

1 Hamlet / Horatio
   Hamlet is Horatio's friend.
2 Claudius / Hamlet
3 Hamlet / Ophelia
4 Laertes and Ophelia / Polonius
5 Hamlet / Gertrude

PRONUNCIATION

⟨ 5 ⟩ Listen and repeat.

1 /s/ Hamlet's girlfriend
2 /z/ Ophelia's brother
3 /ɪz/ Polonius's son

2 **a** Test a partner.
   A Who's Hamlet?
   B He's Horatio's friend and Claudius's nephew.
     Who's ...?

b ⟨ 6 ⟩ Listen. Right ✓ or wrong ✗?
1 *Hamlet is Gertrude's son.* ✓

3 Read about the play. Which character doesn't die at the end?

> Hamlet kills Polonius. Ophelia kills herself. Claudius tries to kill Hamlet with poison but Gertrude drinks it and dies. Laertes, Ophelia's brother, fights Hamlet. Hamlet kills Laertes and Laertes kills Hamlet. But before he dies, Hamlet kills his uncle Claudius.

4 **a** Write five names (friends or family).

b Talk to a partner.
Who's Roberto? How old is he? What does he do?

5 **a** Write *my, his, her, our,* or *their.*

'This is *my* family. Philip's _____ husband. These are _____ children. That's _____ son. _____ name's Charles. And this is _____ daughter. _____ name's Anne. These are Charles's children. _____ names are William and Harry. This is _____ second son. _____ name's Andrew. And these are _____ two children, Eugenie and Beatrice. This is _____ house ...'

b ⟨ 7 ⟩ Listen and check. Who is she?

Irregular plurals		
man	→	men
woman	→	women /wɪmɪn/
person	→	people /piːpl/
child	→	children /tʃɪldrən/
wife	→	wives

Rich woman, poor man

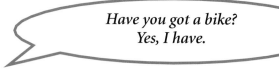

Have you got a bike?
Yes, I have.

1 **a** ◦ 8 ◦ Listen. Tick ✓ or cross ✗ the form.

b Ask a partner. Complete the form.

A Have you got a TV?
B Yes, I have. I've got a Sony. / No, I haven't.

GUARDIAN INSURANCE COMPANY								
Name	📺	📼	💿	📻	📹	⌨️	🚗	🚲
Sue Wright	✓							
_____								

This is **Stan Bowles**, a professional footballer. He plays for England. He'(s)rich and famous. He's got a million pounds in the bank, an expensive car, and a big house in London. He's married and he's got three children. But he's got a big problem – he gambles.

2 **a** ◦ 9 ◦ Read. Tick ✓ or cross ✗ the chart.

1970s	Stan	Anita
1 a lot of money?	✓	✗
2 a job?		
3 a big house?		
4 a wife / husband?		
5 any children?		
6 a small shop?		
7 a big problem?		
8 a good idea?		

b Check your answers with a partner.

A Has Stan got (a lot of money)?
B Yes, he has. / No, he hasn't. Has Anita …?

c Read again. (Circle)'s. Does 's = *is* or *has*?

This is **Anita Roddick**. She's a young housewife. She lives in a small flat in Brighton with her husband, Gordon. They've got two daughters. Anita's got a small shop. She hasn't got any big problems, but she's got a brilliant idea – beauty products with natural ingredients.

GRAMMAR FOCUS 1

have got

● Complete the chart.

+			−		
I you we they	've	got	I (etc.) haven't		got
he she it	's		he (etc.) _____		

?			✓ ✗	
Have I (etc.)		got ...?	Yes, I _____. No, I haven't.	
_____ he (etc.)			Yes, he has. No, he _____.	

Contractions	've = *have*	's = _____
	haven't = _____	hasn't = _____

PRACTICE

a Write sentences.

1 I / fax +   *I've got a fax.*
2 My parents / car −
3 Your brother / mobile phone ?
4 We / yacht +
5 She / microwave −

b Write six true sentences with *have got*.

PRONUNCIATION

a °10°

he   have   how   who   hello   housewife

got   good   green   bag   big   again

b °11° Listen and repeat.

1 He's got an ex<u>pen</u>sive <u>car</u>.
2 They've got <u>two</u> <u>daugh</u>ters.
3 She <u>has</u>n't got any <u>prob</u>lems.
4 I <u>have</u>n't got a <u>job</u>.

3 °12° Listen about Stan and Anita today. Right ✓ or wrong ✗?

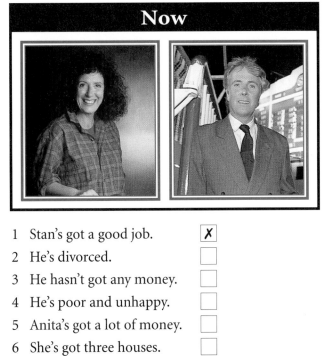

Now

1 Stan's got a good job.   ✗
2 He's divorced.   ☐
3 He hasn't got any money.   ☐
4 He's poor and unhappy.   ☐
5 Anita's got a lot of money.   ☐
6 She's got three houses.   ☐
7 She's got 1,213 shops.   ☐
8 She doesn't like her job.   ☐

GRAMMAR FOCUS 2

some / any

+	Stan's got some problems. (= we don't say how many) Anita's got two children.
−	Anita hasn't got any problems.
?	Has Stan got any children?

● Write *some* or *any*.

Use _____ with plural nouns in + sentences.

Use _____ with plural nouns in ? and − sentences.

PRACTICE

What have you got with you? Write four things.
I've got a / an ... I haven't got a / an ... I've got some ... I haven't got any ...

4 **Small objects** *p.134 Have you got ...?* Ask a partner.

5 Play *I've got ...* Ask the teacher.

like / love / hate + (verb)*-ing*   Activities: *cooking / shopping*, etc.

In your free time

> *She hates cooking and shopping.*

1 ⌈ 13 ⌉ Read the adverts. Write activities A to M.

A *cycling*
B _____
C _____
D _____
E _____
F _____
G _____
H _____
I _____
J _____
K _____
L _____
M _____

1 **Flatmate wanted:** man or woman for a large flat in central Manchester. I'm male, 55, and I'm a retired chef. I smoke and I've got two cats. I love cooking, but I hate shopping! *Box 425.*

2 **Help! Young man needs love.** I'm tall and quite good-looking – I've got long hair and dark brown eyes. I like swimming, cycling, and reading. You're young, fun, and a bit special. Where are you? *Box 101.*

3 **I want a person to travel with me** to South America. I'm female, 34 years old, and I don't smoke. I like skiing, playing cards, dancing, and gardening. What about you? *Box 18.*

4 **My dream man doesn't like watching TV.** He's got short hair and nice eyes. He's tall and he doesn't smoke. He likes listening to good music and going to the cinema and the theatre. He loves travelling to hot countries! Is he only a dream? *Box 271.*

2 Write 1, 2, 3, or 4.

1 Adverts ⌈3⌉ and ⌈ ⌉ are from women.
2 ⌈ ⌉ wants a girlfriend.
3 ⌈ ⌉ and ⌈ ⌉ don't smoke.
4 ⌈ ⌉ likes skiing.
5 ⌈ ⌉ doesn't like long hair.
6 ⌈ ⌉ likes animals.

3 Guess the top three hobbies in Britain.

PRONUNCIATION

a ⌈ 14 ⌉

ŋ   song king going playing swimming cooking

ʊ   cook look put football would good-looking

b ⌈ 15 ⌉ Listen and repeat.
1 I *hate shopping*.

GRAMMAR FOCUS

like / love / hate + (verb)*-ing*

Infinitive	*-ing* form
1 cook	I like cooking.
2 dance	She loves dancing.
3 shop	We hate shopping.

PRACTICE

a Read the adverts again. Find the *-ing* form of these verbs. Are they group **1**, **2**, or **3**?

go   read   watch   travel   swim   cycle   play   ski

b Write five true sentences with *like*, *love*, or *hate*.

4 ⌈ 16 ⌉ Listen to *In your free time*. What does she like / love / hate?

5 Survey. Choose six activities. Interview the teacher and three students. Note the answers.
A Do you like playing chess?
B No, I don't. I hate it!

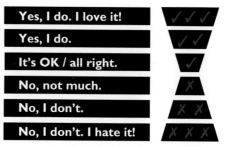

Yes, I do. I love it!   ✓✓✓
Yes, I do.   ✓✓
It's OK / all right.   ✓
No, not much.   ✗
No, I don't.   ✗✗
No, I don't. I hate it!   ✗✗✗

4

D

Tourist shopping

batteries	D	an antique box	☐	a toothbrush	☐	a colour film	☐	*Time* magazine	☐
envelopes	☐	a guide book	☐	stamps	☐	aspirins	☐	postcards	☐

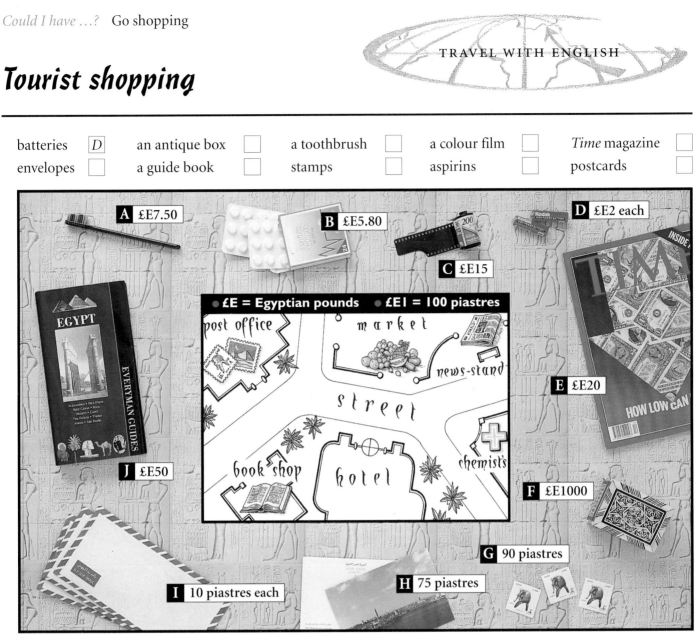

A £E7.50   **B** £E5.80   **C** £E15   **D** £E2 each

E £E20   **J** £E50   **F** £E1000   **G** 90 piastres   **H** 75 piastres   **I** 10 piastres each

● £E = Egyptian pounds   ● £E1 = 100 piastres

post office   market   news-stand   street   book shop   hotel   chemist's

4

1 **a** Match the words and pictures A to J.

  b Use the map. Where can you buy each thing?
  A Where can you buy postcards?
  B At the post office or the news-stand.

2 **a** ॰17॰ Listen. What does she buy? How much are they?

  b Listen again. Number the phrases in the right order (1st to 4th).

Have you got any envelopes?	☐
How much is that?	☐
Could I have ten stamps for Argentina, please?	☐
Do you speak English?	☐

  c In pairs, remember and write the dialogue.

3 ॰18॰ Listen. Copy the intonation.

4 Practise in different shops. Use pictures A to J.
  A You're a shop assistant.
  B You're a tourist. Buy two things. Swap.

5 ॰19॰ Listen to Ana and Riaz shopping. Complete the chart.

Thing(s)	Price
1 _____ / _____	£E _____
2 _____	£E _____
3 _____ / _____	£E _____

6 🛄 **Travel phrasebook 4** *p.130*

Family photos

This is my sister's wedding. That's my sister, Tessa. She's twenty-six. She's very beautiful. She's tall and thin, and she's got green eyes and long dark hair. Next to her is her husband, Paul. He works in Amsterdam. That's my dad, behind Tessa, and my mum's behind Paul. That's Paul's mum between my mum and dad. She's very short! That's me, with long brown hair. That's my wife, Anna, in front of Paul. Anna hates Paul!

A Danny **B** _____ **C** _____ **D** _____ **E** _____ **F** _____ **G** _____

4

1 ⟨20⟩ Read the text. Label the photograph.

2 ✒ **Prepositions of place** _p.140_

The letter _s_ in English
Match five grammatical uses for _s_.
1 I like animals.   a verb _have got_ (_he_ / _she_ / _it_ form)
2 He's an actor.   b possessive '_s_
3 She's got a new car.   c present simple (_he_ / _she_ / _it_ form)
4 Jane's boyfriend.   d plural noun
5 He lives in a flat.   e verb _be_ (_he_ / _she_ / _it_ form)

3 Look at the five _s_ examples in the text. Write a, b, c, d, or e.

1 _sister's_ = b

4 ⟨21⟩ Listen to Danny. Complete the information about his other sister.

Name	Jane
Age	
Married	
Children	
Description	
Job	
Likes	

5 Friend or family? **A** Draw and talk about a person. **B** Ask questions.

Who?

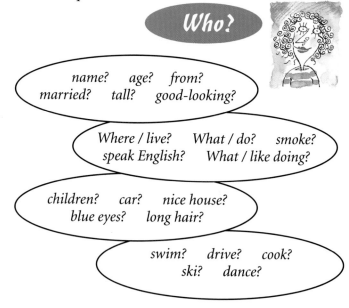

name? age? from?
married? tall? good-looking?

Where / live? What / do? smoke?
speak English? What / like doing?

children? car? nice house?
blue eyes? long hair?

swim? drive? cook?
ski? dance?

⟨22⟩ ♫ _How about you_, Frank Sinatra

⟨23⟩

point boyfriend toilet poison royal unemployed

big brown behind brother beautiful batteries

Vocabulary file 4

1 Word groups Add words for two minutes.

1 Colours *white* …
2 Adjectives *old* …
3 The family *mother* …
4 Possessions *car* …
5 Activities *swimming* …

2 Verbs Match the verbs and phrases.

come cook do hate ~~paint~~ sing want

1 *paint* a picture
2 _____ to English classes
3 _____ sport
4 _____ dinner
5 _____ to learn Chinese
6 _____ a song
7 _____ shopping

3 Opposites Write the missing word.

1 clean   *dirty*
2 Hello   _____
3 finish   _____
4 cold   _____
5 horrible   _____
6 come   _____
7 sit down   _____
8 right   _____

4 Prepositions Complete with behind between in front of .

1 The woman's _____ the man.
2 The man's _____ the woman.
3 The woman's _____ the man and the snake.

5 English sounds Match the pictures and groups 1 to 4.

Circle the different sound.

1 verb learn (like) purple sir word
2 airport hair parents see their there
3 come hungry cousin blue money Monday
4 cook put good-looking room go would

6 Pronunciation ~~Cross out~~ the 'silent' letter(s).
~~know~~ sandwich listen what
write half two answer

7 ✎ **Places B** *p.133* ✎ **Classroom language** at the end of your book.

Study tip
....
■ **Remember words with other words / phrases.**

a Remember words with their opposites.

> ○ *big – opposite = small*
> *My flat isn't big. It's small.*

b Remember words in phrases.

> ○ *sing a song*
> *play basketball*

Try it!
■ Test a partner on exercises 2 and 3.

■ Look at exercise 3 again. Write one for a partner.
....

4

v

Grammar file 4

1 Adjectives (3)

		Adjective	Noun
Singular	It's a	fast	car.
Plural	They're		cars.

She's very tall.
They're quite good-looking.

☐ Adjectives don't change. NOT ~~They're fasts cars.~~
☐ Adjectives go before nouns. NOT ~~It's a car fast.~~

2 Possessive adjectives (2)

I you he she	my your his her	
it	its	Rome is famous for its history.
we	our	We love our dogs.
they	their	Their sister is beautiful.

☐ Possessive adjectives don't change.
   Their daughters are tall. NOT ~~Theirs daughters …~~
☐ *your* (s.) and *your* (pl.) are the same.

3 *have got*

+		
I (etc.)	've	got a phone.
He (etc.)	's	

−		
I (etc.)	haven't	got a phone.
He (etc.)	hasn't	

?		
Have	I (etc.)	got a phone?
Has	he (etc.)	

✓✗		
Yes,	you (etc.)	have. haven't.
No,	he (etc.)	has. hasn't.

Contractions 've = have 's = has
haven't = have not hasn't = has not

Word order in questions

	Verb *have*	Subject	*got*	
	Has	she	got	a car?
How many sisters	have	you	got?	

☐ Use *have got* for things / people.

4 Possessive *'s*

☐ Use *'s* with people.
   NOT ~~He's the boyfriend of my sister.~~
☐ Use *s'* with plurals. NOT ~~It's my parent's house.~~
☐ Use *of* with things. NOT ~~the film's end~~

5 *some / any*

I've got three stamps.
I've got some stamps. (= we don't know how many)

+	some	I've got some aspirins.
−	any	I haven't got any stamps.
?	any	Have you got any envelopes?

☐ *some* = not an exact number.
☐ Use *some / any* + plural nouns.
☐ Use *any* in − and ? .

6 *like / love / hate* + (verb)-*ing*

Infinitive	(verb)-*ing*	Spelling
cook study	I like cooking. She hates studying.	+ ing
dance	We love dancing.	~~e~~ + ing
swim	They love swimming.	1 vowel + 1 consonant → double consonant

☐ Use verb + -*ing* after *like*, *love*, and *hate*.

7 The letter *s* in English

1	Verb *be* (*he / she / it* form)	He's Italian.
2	Verb *have got* (*he / she / it* form)	He's got two children.
3	Plural noun	Their names are Carla and Niki.
4	Possessive *'s*	His wife's name is Alessandra.
5	Present simple (*he / she / it* form)	He lives in Milan.

☐ Remember five grammatical uses for *s* in English.

▶ Workbook *p.52* Do **Grammar check 4**. ▶ **Progress chart** (Files 3 / 4) *p.2*. ▶ Do **Check your progress** *p.51*.

Check your progress

Grammar   Right ✓ = **1** point

1 Write the questions.

like you shopping do? *Do you like shopping?*
1. car a has your got white sister?
2. parents live where your do?
3. brother like music does classical your?
4. finish film what does time the?
5. please small I two could batteries have? ☐ 5

2 Write *a / an* or *some / any*.

I've got *a* credit card.
1. I haven't got _____ children.
2. I've got _____ envelope but I haven't got _____ stamp.
3. We've got _____ very good friends in Cardiff.
4. Do you have _____ single rooms? ☐ 5

3 Write *on, in,* or *at*.
1. The bus leaves *at* 3.30 _____ the afternoon.
2. See you _____ Monday morning _____ 9.15.
3. I work _____ the evening but I don't work _____ night. ☐ 5

4 Write the negatives.

They go to university. *They don't go to university.*
1. My cousin can ski.
2. Her husband speaks English very well.
3. He's got some Turkish cigarettes.
4. The shops open on Saturday afternoon.
5. Our son watches TV every day. ☐ 5

5 Possessive *'s*. Write sentences.

Robin (Kelly) *Robin is Kelly's husband.*

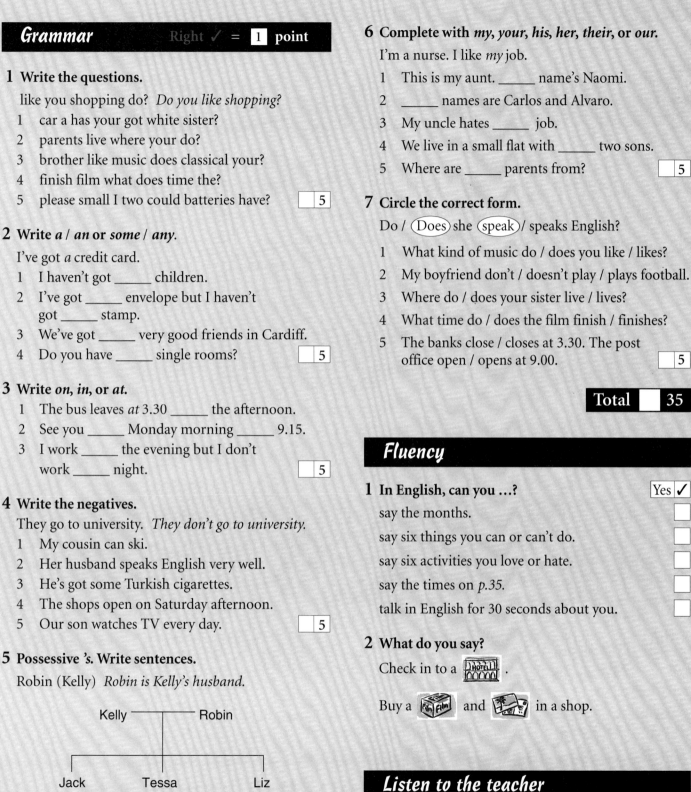

1. Tessa (Kelly)
2. Jack (Liz)
3. Kelly (Robin)
4. Kelly and Robin (Tessa)
5. Jack, Tessa, and Liz (Kelly) ☐ 5

6 Complete with *my, your, his, her, their,* or *our*.

I'm a nurse. I like *my* job.
1. This is my aunt. _____ name's Naomi.
2. _____ names are Carlos and Alvaro.
3. My uncle hates _____ job.
4. We live in a small flat with _____ two sons.
5. Where are _____ parents from? ☐ 5

7 Circle the correct form.

Do / (Does) she (speak) / speaks English?
1. What kind of music do / does you like / likes?
2. My boyfriend don't / doesn't play / plays football.
3. Where do / does your sister live / lives?
4. What time do / does the film finish / finishes?
5. The banks close / closes at 3.30. The post office open / opens at 9.00. ☐ 5

Total ☐ 35

Fluency

1 In English, can you …?   Yes ✓

say the months. ☐
say six things you can or can't do. ☐
say six activities you love or hate. ☐
say the times on *p.35*. ☐
talk in English for 30 seconds about you. ☐

2 What do you say?

Check in to a 🏨 .

Buy a 🎞 and 🖼 in a shop.

Listen to the teacher

1. Write the times.
2. Write six sentences about a mystery woman.
3. Answer the teacher's questions.

Do you live like Suzy Stressed?

She gets up late.

get to work | E
get up late | ☐
get home late | ☐

go to an Italian class | ☐
go to bed late | ☐
go to work | ☐

have dinner | ☐
(not) have breakfast | ☐
have lunch | ☐
have a shower | ☐
have a cigarette / a coffee | ☐

finish work | ☐
use the lift | ☐
watch TV | ☐

5

A

Do you live like this?

1 **a** Match the phrases and pictures A to N.

b ○ 1 ○ Listen. Repeat Suzy Stressed's day.

2 In pairs, describe her day.

A *She gets up late.*

PRONUNCIATION

a ○ 2 ○ Listen and repeat.

/ɪz/

lives	gets	finishes
has	starts	uses
does	smokes	watches

b How do you pronounce these verbs?

goes   works   dances   plays   studies   makes

go running   P

have … for breakfast ☐

do yoga ☐

walk to work ☐

go home ☐

start work ☐

go to bed ☐

get up ☐

have a shower ☐

(not) use the lift ☐

(not) watch TV ☐

3 **a** ° 3 ° This is Henry Healthy's day. Match the phrases and pictures O to Y. Listen and check.

b Answer the questions.

1 What time does he get up? *He gets up at 6.30.*
2 What does he do before breakfast?
3 Does he have a shower?
4 What does he have for breakfast?
5 Does he go to work by car?
6 Does he use the lift?

4 In pairs, find five differences between Suzy and Henry.

Suzy gets up late, but Henry gets up early.

GRAMMAR FOCUS

No article

● Don't use *the* in these phrases.

have	breakfast / lunch / dinner
go / get	to work / school / bed, etc.
	home NOT ~~to home~~
start / finish	work / school, etc.

PRACTICE

Write five true sentences.

I have breakfast at 7.30.

5 🔊 *Have, Go, Get* A *p.141*

6 **a** Does the teacher live like Suzy or like Henry? Ask six questions.

b Ask a partner.

A What time do you get up?
B At (about) 6.45. / It depends.
A Do you have …?

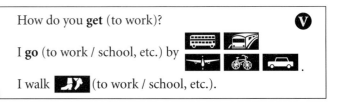

How do you **get** (to work)?	▼
I **go** (to work / school, etc.) by	
I walk 👣 (to work / school, etc.).	

7 Survey. How do you get to work / school / class?

A How do you get (to class)?
B I (walk). How do you …?

How to live to be 100!

> *I always drive. I never walk.*

★ How the stars stay young ★

This week's star is ... Liz Taylor. Here are her secrets.

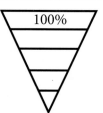

100%

0%

She *always* drinks fifteen glasses of water a day.
She _____ has juice, grapefruit, and water for breakfast.
She *often* eats fresh fruit and vegetables.
She _____ does aerobics and swims a kilometre a day.
She *hardly ever* eats meat.
She _____ smokes, or has caffeine, sugar, or salt.

But if you ask Liz her number one secret, she smiles and says it's her love of life.

HOW TO LIVE TO BE 100!

DO YOU ...?

I	**have breakfast** A never / hardly ever B sometimes C usually
2	**have three meals a day** A never / hardly ever B sometimes C usually
3	**eat fresh fruit and vegetables** A never / hardly ever B sometimes C often
4	**eat fried food (chips, etc.)** A often B sometimes C never / hardly ever
5	**put salt on your food** A always B sometimes C never / hardly ever
6	**drink alcohol** A often B sometimes C never / hardly ever
7	**take sugar in tea / coffee** A always B sometimes C never
8	**do exercise** A never / hardly ever B sometimes C often

9	**travel by car** A usually B sometimes C never / hardly ever
10	**feel tired or stressed** A always B sometimes C never / hardly ever
11	**go out with friends** A never / hardly ever B sometimes C often

HOW MANY ...?

12	**hours do you sleep a day** A 0 – 4 B 5 – 6 C 7 – 9
13	**cigarettes do you smoke a day** A 10+ B 0 – 10 C none
14	**cups of tea / coffee do you have a day** A 3+ B 1 – 2 C none
15	**hours do you work / study a week** A 50+ B 35 – 50 C 0 – 35

Score: A = 3   B = 5   C = 7
Total score = number of years to live!

5

B

1 Read about Liz. Complete with *never*, *sometimes*, and *usually*.

PRONUNCIATION

○ **4** ○ Listen. Repeat the sentences about Liz.

GRAMMAR FOCUS

Adverbs of frequency: *always* / *usually*, etc.

● Look at the text again. (Circle) the right rule.
Adverbs of frequency go **before** / **after** the verb.

PRACTICE

a Do the questionnaire **How to live to be 100!**

b Check your score. What does it mean?

2 **a** Write six sentences about your lifestyle.
I hardly ever use lifts.

b Play *Guess who?* with the sentences.

3 ○ **5** ○ Read and answer.

1 Which **Top Ten Rules** do you break?
2 Which do you think are the top three?

The Top Ten Rules
Scientists believe that if we follow ten rules we can easily live to be 100.

1	**Breakfast**	Always start the day with a good breakfast.
2	**Three meals**	Always eat three meals a day.
3	**Diet**	Eat well! Eat a lot of fresh fruit and vegetables, fish, and chicken. Don't eat a lot of meat. Never eat fried food. Don't put sugar in your tea or coffee.
4	**Alcohol**	Don't drink a lot of alcohol (but a glass of wine sometimes with a meal is OK).
5	**Coffee**	Don't drink a lot of coffee.
6	**Cigarettes**	Every cigarette you smoke shortens your life. Stop smoking today!
7	**Social life**	People with a good social life often live longer. Married people usually live a long time. Don't stay at home! Go out! Get married!
8	**Exercise**	Do exercise or sport often to live longer.
9	**Sleep**	Sleep seven or eight hours a day.
10	**Stress**	Stress kills! Don't worry. Relax!

4 Guess which rules the teacher breaks. Ask questions to check.

How do you study?

5 **a** Add an adverb of frequency to make true sentences.

<pre>   often
1 I / listen to English cassettes.</pre>

2 I study the Grammar files.

3 I use a dictionary.

4 I do homework.

5 I read magazines in English.

6 I revise before lessons.

7 I speak English in class.

8 I use English outside class.

9 I listen to English songs.

10 I record myself on a cassette.

b Compare in groups. Which things do you never do? Why not?

○ **6** ○

 here we're year really theatre engineer

she fresh sugar station social information

A weekend in Spain

> How often do you go to the cinema?
> About once a month.

1 **a** 📖 *Have, Go, Get* **B** *p.141*

  b *Do you often go …? Ask a partner.*

2 **a** Right ✓ or wrong ✗? What do you think?

  1 The Spanish have lunch and dinner early. ☐
  2 The Spanish sleep a lot. ☐
  3 The Spanish don't often go out. ☐

  b Read paragraph 1. Check your answers.

  c Where do you think Spanish people go on Fridays and Saturdays? Write four places. Read paragraph 2 to check.

  d Read paragraph 3. Write three things they do on Sundays.

☾ THE COUNTRY ☀
☀ THAT NEVER SLEEPS ☽

1 SPAIN is famous for its unusual lifestyle. For example, Spanish people usually have lunch at 2.30 p.m. and dinner at 10.00 p.m. People don't usually go to bed before midnight. Visitors to Spain often ask, 'When do Spanish people sleep?' The Spanish sleep less and go out more than other Europeans.

2 THE Spanish love walking, and they often go for a walk around the town in the evenings. At 10.00 on Friday and Saturday nights the bars and restaurants are full. The cinema is very popular in Spain (25% of adults go to the cinema once a week or more). But Spanish night-life really starts at midnight. A lot of disco-bars don't close before 6.00 in the morning. In Valencia, on the east coast of Spain, some discos open at 10.00 on Sunday mornings!

3 ONLY about 21% of the population go to church. On Sundays many people go to the country or to the beach. Spanish people often go away at weekends, at Easter, and at Christmas. Many families have a house in the country, and go there in the summer. People often sit in traffic jams on Sunday evenings. And on 1st August, twelve million cars are on the road!

──────────── ☾ ☀ ☽ ────────────

3 a Correct these sentences.

1 The Spanish go for a walk around the town in the mornings.
They go for a walk around the town in the evenings.

2 The restaurants and bars are full every night.

3 The discos and bars close at 11.00 p.m.

4 The Spanish often drive to the beach on Sunday evenings.

5 The Spanish hardly ever go away at Easter or Christmas.

b What do you do at weekends?

GRAMMAR FOCUS 1

Prepositions of time: *in / on / at*

● Look at the text. Write *in*, *on*, and *at* in the right columns.

_____	_____	
lunchtime	the morning(s), etc.	Sunday(s)
2.30	(the) summer	Saturday night(s)
midnight		1st August
Easter / Christmas		
weekends		
night		

PRACTICE

Ask a partner.

A When do you relax?

B At weekends and in the evenings. / It depends. When do you …?

come to English class · go out · go shopping · go away · relax · study · have coffee · ?

4 ° 7 ° Listen to Teresa Pons from Valencia. Complete the sentences with *once*, *twice*, *every*, or a number.

1 She goes to the cinema *three* or _____ times a month.

2 She goes to a disco _____ or _____ times a month.

3 She goes to dance classes _____ or _____ a week.

4 She goes to church _____ Sunday.

5 She goes away at weekends _____ or _____ times a year.

6 She goes for a walk nearly _____ day.

GRAMMAR FOCUS 2

Expressions of frequency

How often (do you …)?		
(about)	once twice three times	a day / a week / a month / a year
	every	day / night / Saturday / week

PRACTICE

Write six true sentences.
My son goes to the cinema once a week.

PRONUNCIATION

° 8 ° Listen and repeat.

1 I <u>go</u> to the <u>cinema</u> <u>twice</u> a <u>week</u>.

2 She <u>goes</u> for a <u>walk</u> in the <u>evenings</u>.

3 He <u>never</u> <u>goes</u> <u>out</u> at <u>night</u>.

4 They <u>often</u> <u>drive</u> to the <u>beach</u> at week<u>ends</u>.

5 ▶◀ *How often do you …?* **A** *p.119* **B** *p.122*

° 9 °

ʧ	ten · time · stop · night · city · lifestyle
aʊ	our · out · how · town · house · sound

Dear Anneka ...

Václav, 45, wants to write to other English students. His hobbies are cooking, sport, and computer games. PO Box 248, Prague, Czech Republic.

Anneka Johnsson, 21, wants a penfriend. She likes travelling, films, and music. PO Box 351, Stockholm, Sweden.

1 What do you need to write in English? Tick ✓.

business letters	☐	exercises	☐
letters to friends	☐	compositions	☐
faxes	☐	a diary	☐
postcards	☐	other (what?)	☐
birthday cards	☐		

Tip 1

When you write a letter or composition:

a write (or type) a 'draft' – don't worry about mistakes.

b have a break when you finish.

....

2 Read Marcia's draft letter in one minute. What can you remember about her?

Avenida Angélica 240
Apto. 3A
São Paulo
Brazil
12th August, 1995

Dear Anneka,
1 My name's Marcia. I'm ᴮbrazilian. I'm from Santos. Is a modern city in the south of Brazil. I'm 23 years old. I'm divorced and I live with my parents. We've got a flat small near the beach.

2 I'm travel agent and I work in an office in São Paulo. São Paulo's very big and noisy but I like it. I speak Portuguese and a little Spanish. I go to English classes at the university twice a week. My teacher say my English is quite good. What do you think.

Tip 2

....

Read your draft again carefully.

a Check each sentence. Highlight and correct any mistakes.

b Check spelling and punctuation (e.g. capital letters, full stops, etc.).

....

3 **a** In pairs, correct the mistakes in paragraphs 1 and 2. Are the mistakes grammar (G), spelling (S), or punctuation (P)?

b Find seven mistakes in the rest of the letter. Are they G, S, or P?

Tip 3

....

When you think your draft is OK, write a clean copy.

....

4 Write a letter to Marcia, Anneka, or Václav. Follow tips 1 to 3. Then give it to the teacher.

3 I haven't got some brothers or sisters but I've got a young son. His name's Gilberto and he's four years. He's lovely!

4 I need English for my job. I want go to the USA to learn English but I can't leave Gilberto and it's very expansive.

5 I like read and listening to music. At weekends, I usually play volleyball and I go often dancing. I love samba!

6 Life in sweden must be very interesting.
Please write to me soon.

Best wishes,

Marcia

PS Please send a photo!

5

At the restaurant

RESTAURANT *Maxwell's*

Special lunch menu
Only $25
(Not including drinks or service)

Starter
Garlic mushrooms
Vegetable soup

Main course
Cheese omelette and salad
Steak and chips
Seafood pasta

Dessert
Strawberries and ice-cream
Chocolate mousse

5

WAITER	Good afternoon, madam, sir.
ZARINA	A table for two, please.
WAITER	Yes, come this way.
WAITER	Are you ready to order now?
ALEX	Yes, I'd like *garlic* _____, please.
ZARINA	Could I have _____ _____ ?
WAITER	And for your main course?
ALEX	I'd like _____ _____.
ZARINA	_____ _____ for me, please.
WAITER	Anything to drink?
ZARINA	A large bottle of _____ _____.
WAITER	Would you like anything else?
ZARINA	Two _____, please, and could we have the bill?
ZARINA	Can I pay by credit card?
WAITER	Yes, of course.

p.m.

1 [a] ◦10◦ Listen. What do they order? Complete the dialogue.

[b] Listen and repeat. Write a word or draw a picture next to each line to help you remember it.

[c] Cover the dialogue. Practise in threes with your words / pictures.

2 [a] ◦11◦ Listen to three more customers. On the menu, tick ✓ the food you hear.

[b] Look at their bill. Is it right?

[c] ◦12◦ Listen and check.

3 x Special menu	$75
3 x drinks	$12
3 x coffees	$9
Total	**$96**

3 Role-play in threes. **A** You're a waiter. **B** and **C** You're customers.

4 📖 **Travel phrasebook 5** *p.130*

Contraction   I'd = I would

59

The perfect time-manager?

A DAY IN THE LIFE OF
Mark McCormack, multi-millionaire

1 Mark McCormack is American. He's sixty-three. He's the manager of many famous people, including the Pope, Monica Seles, and Alain Prost. He's married with two sons and a daughter. He has forty-two offices in twenty countries, and homes in London, New York, Cleveland, and Florida.

2 I get up every morning at 4.30. If my notebook says 'Do exercise', I do some exercise. My secretary arrives at about 5.15, and she brings the newspaper. Then I have a shower and I get dressed. I usually have coffee and cereal for breakfast at the Carlton Tower Hotel (if I am with a client) or I just have a coffee at home.

3 First I look at my yellow notebook. On the left are my meetings, on the right are my phonecalls. I'm a very good time-manager. I always plan my life exactly for the next six months. I write down everything I do: how many hours I sleep, how many hours I see my children, and how many hours I spend in each city in the world. I have business meetings in my office from 9.00 a.m. until lunchtime. At 1.00 I usually have lunch at the Carlton, and I always sit at the same table. After lunch I call the USA, and after that I sleep until 6.00.

4 At 7.00 I often have a drink with a friend or client in the bar. I usually have a Jack Daniels whisky. Then I have dinner at a restaurant. I never cook. In the evening, if my wife is with me, we sometimes go to the cinema. We have meetings to plan our life together. We try to spend about 60% of our time together. I go to bed at about 11.30. Sleeping is not a problem for me. It's in my yellow notebook – so I go to bed and I sleep.

Notes

April 19th		☎
a.m.		
2		
4	4.45 Do exercise	
6		
8	8.10 Meet Jan/Carlton	
10		10.35 John
12		
p.m.	1.00 Lunch – Kiri	
2		2.30 USA – Agassi
4		4.10 Italy
6	Sleep	
8	8.15 Betsy – bar	
10		
	11.30 🛏 !	
12		

1 **a** Look at the photo. Write six questions about Mark McCormack.

~~age~~   nationality   marital status   children
job   live

1 *How old is he?*

b Read paragraph 1 quickly. Check your answers.

2 Read paragraph 2. Circle the right answer.
1 His secretary is a man / woman.
2 He has a shower before / after breakfast.
3 He always / never has coffee for breakfast.

3 Read paragraph 3. Right ✓ or wrong ✗?
1 He plans his life very carefully. ☐
2 He writes down everything he does. ☐
3 He usually has lunch at home. ☐
4 He doesn't work in the afternoon. ☐

4 **a** Imagine three things he does in the evenings.
Read paragraph 4 and check.

b Do you like his lifestyle?

Then / After that / After …		
I have lunch.	**Then** **After lunch** **After that** NOT ~~After~~	I have coffee.

5 Complete the paragraph.

about   after (x 2)   at   ~~for~~   from   in
then (x 2)   until

He gets up early and usually does some exercise. He works with his secretary and assistant *for* two hours, and _____ he has breakfast _____ 8.30. He has meetings all morning _____ 9.00 _____ lunchtime. _____ lunch he calls the USA. _____ he sleeps until 6.00. _____ the evening he has drinks and dinner in the hotel. _____ dinner he sometimes meets his wife and sees a film. He goes to bed at _____ 11.30.

6 Play *Memory test*. Ask the teacher questions about the text.

7 **a** Do the **Questionnaire**. Tick ✓ your answers.

b Interview a partner. Cross ✗ his / her answers. Are you both good time-managers?

◦13◦ ♫ *Anything you want*, Roy Orbison

◦14◦

 chair   change   lunch   watch   children   picture

 age   say   day   late   famous   eighty

Questionnaire	Are you a good time-manager?					
How often do you …?	always	usually	often	sometimes	hardly ever	never
1 plan your day						
2 write things in your diary						
3 arrive late						
4 forget things						
5 look at your watch						
6 have time to relax						
How often do you say …?	always	usually	often	sometimes	hardly ever	never
7 'I'm sorry I'm late.'						
8 'I haven't got time.'						
9 'Oh, no! Look at the time!'						
10 'Good. I'm early.'						

Vocabulary file 5

1 Puzzle Write the next word.

1 Sunday Monday *Tuesday*
2 first second _____
3 second minute _____
4 three times twice _____
5 starter main course _____
6 autumn winter _____

2 Verbs Complete the phrases.

1 n *e e* d to learn English / a new car
2 l _ _ e your wallet / some money
3 g _ to school / for a walk
4 h _ _ e a bath / eggs for breakfast
5 f _ _ _ _ h work / an exercise
6 u _ _ a computer / the lift
7 g _ _ to work / up late

3 Adverbs Find the words.

1 sulylau   *usually*
2 tnofe   _____
3 steimsmeo   _____
4 vreen   _____
5 syawla   _____

4 Routines Order your typical day (1st to 10th).

1 go to work   ☐   6 have dinner   ☐
2 get up   ☐   7 finish work   ☐
3 have breakfast ☐   8 go to bed   ☐
4 start work   ☐   9 have lunch   ☐
5 go home   ☐   10 do exercise   ☐

5 Prepositions Complete with after before by from like until.

1 Do you live _____ Suzy or Henry?
2 _____ breakfast I go to work.
3 They come to class _____ bus.
4 He studies _____ 9.30 _____ 5.45.
5 She has a shower _____ she goes to bed.

6 English sounds Put the words in the right group.

about engineer brown oil hear toilet here
hour royal pound point idea

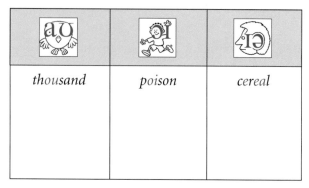

aʊ	ɔɪ	ɪə
thousand	*poison*	*cereal*

7 🔊 Food and drink B *p.135* 🔊 *Have, Go, Get* C *p.141*

Study tip

■ **Experiment! Remember words in different ways.**

a Write words on cards. Test yourself.

b Write a personal example.

beach – I love going to the beach! My favourite beach is 'Il Lido'.

c Draw a picture.

The beach

d Imagine the word.

Try it!

■ Choose ten words from File 5. Remember them in different ways.

■ How do you learn new words?

Grammar file 5

1 Present simple: routines

She gets up at 7.30 every day. Then she has a shower.
We have dinner at 6.00. After that we watch TV.

☐ Use the present simple for things you do every
day / week, etc.

☐ Remember: After **that** we … / After **dinner** we …
NOT ~~After we watch TV.~~

2 No article

I	have	breakfast / lunch / dinner	at 7.00.
	go get	to work / school / bed	
	start finish	work / school	
	go home		

☐ Don't use *the* with *have* (*breakfast* / *lunch*, etc.).
NOT ~~I have the dinner.~~

☐ Don't use *the* with verbs + *work* / *school* / *bed*.
NOT ~~I go to the bed.~~

☐ Don't use *the* or *to* with *go home*.
NOT ~~I go to the home.~~

☐ Don't use *the* when you speak about things in general.
I like **music**. NOT ~~I like the music.~~

3 Expressions of frequency

Adverbs

I	always usually often sometimes hardly ever never	have breakfast.	100% 0%

		Adverb	Verb	
I What time do you		never usually	go finish	to the cinema. work?

☐ Adverbs of frequency go before the verb.

☐ Adverbs of frequency go after *be*.
NOT ~~He always is tired.~~

How often …?

How often do you	cook?	
	go to the theatre?	

I cook I go to the theatre	(about)	once twice three times four times	a	day. week. month. year.
		every		evening. day. week, etc.

☐ Use *once* / *twice*. NOT ~~one time / two times~~

4 *have* or *have got*?

Things / People

I have / don't have I've got / haven't got	a car. two children.

Activities

I have / don't have	breakfast a shower	at 6.00.

☐ Use *have* or *have got* for things / people.
(*Do you have …?* = *Have you got …?*)

☐ Use only *have* for activities.
NOT ~~I've got a shower at 6.00.~~

5 Prepositions of time (2)

in	on	at
the morning the afternoon the evening December the summer	Monday (morning) 1st May	six o'clock night lunchtime Christmas the weekend

☐ Use *in* for parts of the day, months, and seasons.

☐ Use *on* for days and dates.

☐ Use *at* for times of the day and festivals.

5

G

▶ Workbook *p.53* Do **Grammar check 5**.

Only rock 'n roll, but I like it

> **What do you think of the Rolling Stones?**
> **I love them. They're great.**

NIGEL What do you *think* of Dolly Parton?
JULIAN I don't _____ her. She's _____.
NIGEL Do you like Bob Dylan?
JULIAN No, I don't.
NIGEL Why _____?
JULIAN Because he's an old hippie!
NIGEL Oh, I _____ him. I think his songs are _____.
JULIAN What about Dire Straits?
NIGEL No, I _____ them. They're _____.

6

A

1 ◦1◦ Listen to *Is it a hit?* Write positive ➕ or negative ➖. <u>Underline</u> the stress.

<u>te</u>rrible	➖	nothing special	☐
boring	☐	great	☐
very good	☐	brilliant	☐
interesting	☐	awful	☐

2 a ◦2◦ Listen. What kind of music is it?

blues   classical   country and western
jazz   opera   pop   rock

b Listen again. What do you think of the music?
I (don't) like it. It's (terrible).

3 a ◦3◦ Listen. Which CD does Nigel choose?

b Listen again. Complete the dialogue.

GRAMMAR FOCUS

Object pronouns: *me / him*, etc.

> I like Pavarotti. Do you like him?
>
> 'What do you think of Dire Straits?' 'I hate them.'

● Look at the dialogue. Complete the chart.

Pronoun	I	you	he	she	it	we	they
Object pronoun	me	you	____	____	it	us	____

PRACTICE

Complete the sentences.

1   I love you. Do you love *me*?
2   We don't understand. Can you help _____?
3   Where's your sister? I need to speak to _____.
4   'What do you think of my new jeans?' 'I don't like _____.'
5   'Do you like Bruce Springsteen?' 'Yes, I like _____ very much.'

PRONUNCIATION

◦4◦ Listen. Repeat sentences 1 to 5.

4 Talk about the musicians in the picture.

5 ▶◀ *What do you think of …?* **A** and **B** *p.119*

My favourite room

Are there any pictures in the room?

The flat's (on) the fifth floor. This is the living-room. It's quite large. There are three big windows, so it's very light. The plant next to the piano is very happy. There are some flowers in a vase on the small table near the window, and some more in another vase on the piano.

There's a beautiful light-blue carpet on the floor. There aren't any chairs, but there are two large dark blue sofas. Between them, there's a glass coffee table, and a small light-blue stool. There's another long stool under the piano. And there are some lovely Indian cushions on the sofas.

The walls are white, and there aren't any pictures in the room. There are some shelves in the corner. There isn't a television in this room, because the piano is here.

The furniture is modern. The tall lamp behind the plant and the small lamp on the coffee table are both new. There aren't a lot of small things in the room, only the two ashtrays.

A c *o r n e r*
B p _ _ _ _
C l _ _ _
D v _ _ _
E c _ _ _ _ _
F a _ _ _ _ _ _
G s _ _ _ _
H s _ _ _
I c _ _ _ _ _ _

1 a ° 5 ° Read. (Circle) the prepositions.

b Complete words A to I. Test a partner.

2 Right ✓ or wrong ✗?

1 There are three plants in the room. ✗
2 There are four shelves in the corner. ☐
3 There's a clock on the shelf. ☐
4 There are some pictures on the wall. ☐
5 There aren't any cushions on the floor. ☐
6 There isn't a lamp in the room. ☐

3 a What do you think of the room?

b ° 6 ° 🎵 Whose room is it? Listen and check.

GRAMMAR FOCUS

There is / are + a / an / some / any

● Complete the chart.

Singular		Plural
+ There's a TV.		There _____ some plants.
− There _____ a TV.		There aren't _____ plants.
? Is _____ a TV?		_____ there any plants?
✓ ✗ Yes, there _____. No, _____ isn't.		Yes, _____ are. No, there _____.

PRACTICE

A Write five sentences about the room. **B** Say right ✓ or wrong ✗.

PRONUNCIATION

° 7 ° Listen. Repeat the grammar chart.

4 Play *Test your memory*. Ask the teacher.

5 📖 House **B** *p.138*

6 ►◄ **Find ten differences A** *p.120* **B** *p.122*

6

B

Murder at Christmas 1

> *Were you alone at 7.00 yesterday?*
> *No, I wasn't.*

1 Read the newspaper article. What happened on Christmas Day, 1948?

2 **a** Read about the suspects. Match the people and photos A to F.

   b ° 8 ° Listen. Who finds the body?

3 **a** ° 9 ° Listen and answer.

   1 Where was Tony at 7.00?
   2 Who was he with?

   b Listen again. Complete the dialogue.

MURDER OF MILLIONAIRE NEWSPAPER 'KING'

Tuesday December 27th 1948
● Last Sunday was James Harvey's last Christmas lunch. At 7.00 p.m., at a family party in his house in the country, somebody murdered him. There were six people in the house. The police …

The suspects

A   Ingrid

B _____

C   Simon

D _____

E _____

F _____

Alison Harvey
Harvey's wife. She hates her husband.

Tony and Simon
Harvey's two sons. They hate their father.

Sally Buxton
Harvey's beautiful secretary and ex-lover.

Geoffrey Smith
Harvey's business partner. They are not friends.

Ingrid Harvey
Harvey's daughter. She's in love with Geoffrey.

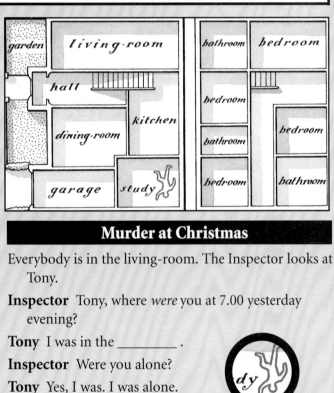

Murder at Christmas

Everybody is in the living-room. The Inspector looks at Tony.

Inspector   Tony, where *were* you at 7.00 yesterday evening?

Tony   I was in the _____ .

Inspector   Were you alone?

Tony   Yes, I was. I was alone.
    (He looks out of the window.)

Inspector   Are you sure?

Tony   Yes, Inspector. I was alone.

Sally   (angrily) No, you weren't, Tony. Tell him the truth.

Tony   All right, Inspector. I wasn't in the _____ .
    I was upstairs … in my _____ .

Inspector   And who were you with?

Tony   (quietly) I was … I was with _____ .

6
C

GRAMMAR FOCUS

Verb *be*: past simple

● Complete with *was*, *were*, *wasn't*, or *weren't*.

+	I (He / She / It) was	You (We / They) were	at home.
−	I (etc.) _____	You (etc.) _____	
?	_____ I (etc.)	_____ you (etc.)	at the cinema?
✓✗	Yes, I _____. No, I _____.	Yes, you (etc.) _____. No, you (etc.) _____.	

Contractions was not = _____	_____ = weren't

PRONUNCIATION

⟨10⟩ Listen and repeat.

1 /wəz/   <u>Where</u> was <u>Sa</u>lly? <u>She</u> was with <u>To</u>ny.
2 /wə/   <u>Where</u> were <u>To</u>ny and <u>Sa</u>lly? <u>They</u> were in <u>To</u>ny's room.
3 /wɒz/   <u>Yes</u>, I <u>was</u>. <u>No</u>, I <u>was</u>n't. I <u>was</u>n't in the <u>gar</u>den.
4 /wɜː/   <u>Yes</u>, they <u>were</u>. <u>No</u>, they <u>weren't</u>. They <u>weren't</u> at <u>home</u>.

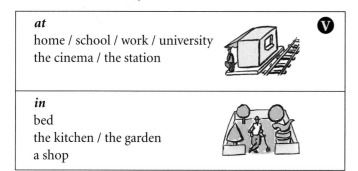

at
home / school / work / university
the cinema / the station
Ⓥ

in
bed
the kitchen / the garden
a shop

4 **a** Where were you yesterday at these times?

7.00 a.m.   10.45 a.m.   2.15 p.m.   4.30 p.m.   7.55 p.m.   12.20 a.m.

1 *I was in bed at 7.00 a.m.*

b Survey. Were you in the same place at the same time?
A Where were you at 7.00 yesterday morning?
B I was in / at …

5 📖 **Places** *p.133 Were you at / in … yesterday / last night / this morning?*
Ask a partner.

⟨11⟩

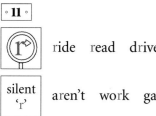

(r) ride read drive three sorry tomorrow

silent 'r' — aren't work garden person upstairs yesterday

PRACTICE
Write past simple sentences.

1	I'm tired. *I was tired.*
2	It's Tuesday.
3	They aren't happy.
4	He isn't in Scotland.
5	Is she at home?
6	Are you angry?
7	We aren't married.

6
C

Murder at Christmas 2

> Were there any clues in the room?
> Yes, there were.

Inspector Now, tell me Mrs Harvey, what time *was* it?

Alison It _____ about 7.15. (crying) My husband _____ on the floor. It _____ horrible! There _____ some papers on the floor, too.

Inspector _____ there any papers in his hand?

Alison No, there _____.

Inspector _____ there anything else?

Alison No, there _____ … Oh! Yes, there was. There _____ a whisky glass on the table.

Inspector _____ that unusual?

Alison Yes, my husband doesn't – didn't – drink whisky, Inspector.

Inspector And where _____ you at 7.00?

Alison I _____ in the living-room, with Simon.

1 Describe the study.
There are some papers on the floor.

2 **a** ° 12 ° Listen. What was unusual in the room?

b Listen again. Complete the dialogue with *was*, *wasn't*, *were*, or *weren't*.

GRAMMAR FOCUS

There was / were

● Write past simple sentences.

+	There's a knife in his back. *There was a knife in his back.* There are some papers on the floor. _____
−	There isn't a gun on the floor. _____ There aren't any papers in his hand. _____

PRACTICE

Write six questions about the room. Ask a partner.
Was there a knife on the floor?

3 ►◄ Murder! **A** *p.120* **B** *p.122* **C** *p.123*

4 **a** Where were the suspects at seven o'clock? Read the dialogues (Files 6C/6D) again. Complete the chart for Tony, Sally, and Alison.

	Where?	Who with?
Tony	*in his room*	
Sally		
Alison		
Simon		
Ingrid		
Geoffrey		

b ° 13 ° Listen. Complete the rest of the chart.

5 ° 14 ° Who was the murderer? Guess. Listen to the end of the story. Were you right?

At tourist information

TRAVEL WITH ENGLISH

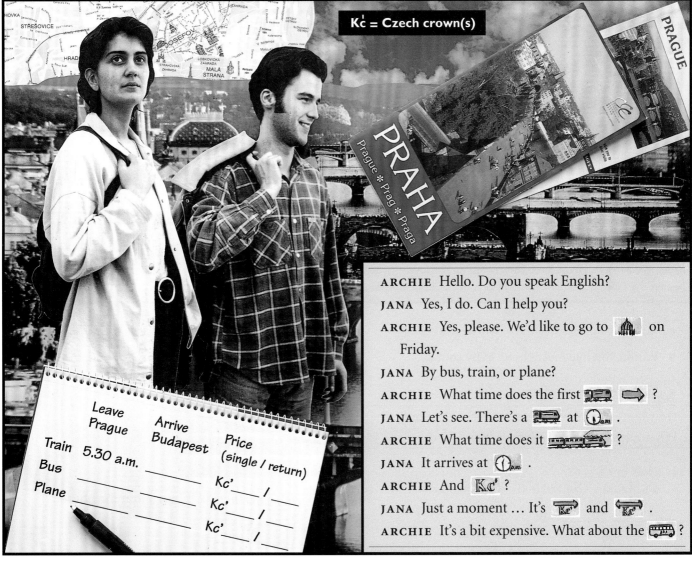

Kč = Czech crown(s)

PRAHA — Prague * Prag * Praha

PRAGUE

ARCHIE Hello. Do you speak English?

JANA Yes, I do. Can I help you?

ARCHIE Yes, please. We'd like to go to 🏛 on Friday.

JANA By bus, train, or plane?

ARCHIE What time does the first 🚂 ➡ ?

JANA Let's see. There's a 🚆 at ①am .

ARCHIE What time does it 🚆 ?

JANA It arrives at ①p.m. .

ARCHIE And Kč ?

JANA Just a moment … It's Kč and Kč .

ARCHIE It's a bit expensive. What about the 🚌 ?

	Leave Prague	Arrive Budapest	Price (single / return)
Train	5.30 a.m.	_____	Kč'___ / ___
Bus	_____	_____	Kč'___ / ___
Plane	_____	_____	Kč'___ / ___

1 **a** ⚬15⚬ Listen. Complete his notes about trains.

  b Listen and repeat. Practise in pairs.

2 **a** ⚬16⚬ Listen. Complete Archie's notes about buses and planes.

  b ⚬17⚬ Listen. How do they travel? Why?

3 Role-play *A weekend away*. Ask the teacher.

4 **a** Look at photos A to F. Ask and answer in pairs.

  A Where were they at a quarter past six?

  B They were …

  b ⚬18⚬ Listen to four dialogues. Match them to the photos.

A 6.15 a.m.

B 12.50 a.m.

C 2.00 p.m.

D 4.45 p.m.

E 6.30 p.m. — 1600 Ft

F 8.20 p.m.

5 📖 **Travel phrasebook 6** *p.131*

House for sale

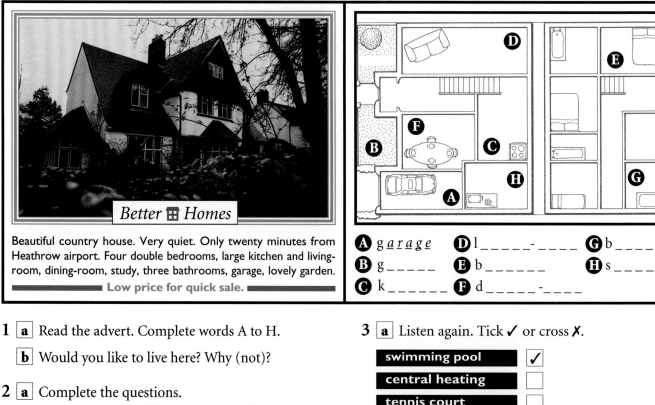

Better ⊞ Homes

Beautiful country house. Very quiet. Only twenty minutes from Heathrow airport. Four double bedrooms, large kitchen and living-room, dining-room, study, three bathrooms, garage, lovely garden.
▬▬▬▬▬ Low price for quick sale. ▬▬▬▬▬

Ⓐ g _a r a g e_   Ⓓ l _ _ _ _ _ - _ _ _ _   Ⓖ b _ _ _ _ _ _ _

Ⓑ g _ _ _ _ _   Ⓔ b _ _ _ _ _ _   Ⓗ s _ _ _ _

Ⓒ k _ _ _ _ _ _   Ⓕ d _ _ _ _ _ - _ _ _ _

6

◁▷

1 ⓐ Read the advert. Complete words A to H.

ⓑ Would you like to live here? Why (not)?

2 ⓐ Complete the questions.

How big How many ~~How much~~ How old
What time Where Why Which

1 *How much* is it?
   a £14,000   **ⓑ** £140,000   **c** £400,000

2 _____ is it?
   a very big   **b** quite big   **c** small

3 _____ rooms has it got?
   a 9   **b** 10   **c** 11

4 _____ is it?
   a in the country   **b** in a town   **c** in a city

5 _____ is it?
   a 19   **b** 90   **c** 190 years old

6 _____ is she interested in the house?
   Because it's **a** cheap   **b** old   **c** near Oxford

7 _____ day can she see the house?
   a Tuesday   **b** Friday   **c** Thursday

8 _____ can she see the house?
   a at 5.45   **b** at 6.45   **c** at 7.45

ⓑ ｜°**19**°｜ Listen. Circle a, b, or c.

3 ⓐ Listen again. Tick ✓ or cross ✗.

swimming pool	✓
central heating	
tennis court	
furniture	
phone	
sauna	

ⓑ Tell a partner six things about the house.
1 *There's a swimming pool.*

4 ｜°**20**°｜ Listen. Which rooms do they go in? Do they want to buy the house?

5 ►◄ **Sell your house** A *p.120* B *p.123*

6 Write about your ideal house.
   My ideal house is in … It's got … There's / There are …

｜°**21**°｜

low   old   go   no   home   smoke

usually   unusual   garage   revision

Vocabulary file 6

1 Word groups Add ten words from the square.

```
T  R  E  C  O  B  K
L  C  A  R  P  E  T
S  B  H  E  R  D  E
C  O  O  K  E  R  R
B  R  P  I  U  O  R
L  I  E  T  U  O  I
U  N  R  C  L  M  B
E  G  A  H  I  M  L
S  P  H  E  M  X  E
B  C  L  N  O  Q  F
```

1 Furniture *sofa* …
2 Rooms *dining-room* …
3 Music *rock* …
4 Object pronouns *me* …
5 Adjectives *brilliant* …

2 Puzzle Write the missing word(s).

1 bedroom / sleep   kitchen / *cook*
2 secretary / works student / _____
3 this / here   that / _____
4 seven days / a week sixty seconds / _____
5 carpet / floor   shelf / _____
6 we / us   they / _____
7 is / was   are / _____

3 Verbs Match the verbs and phrases.

call change go enjoy make ~~put~~

1 *put* sugar in tea / something in your pocket
2 _____ money / traveller's cheques
3 _____ a film / reading
4 _____ a friend / the police
5 _____ to the beach / swimming
6 _____ a pizza / a reservation

4 Prepositions Complete with at in of near

1 The end _____ the film.
2 He's _____ bed / the kitchen / the car.
3 She's _____ home / work / school.
4 Do you live _____ the station?

5 Places Where can you …

1 buy stamps? *at a post office*
2 get a bus? _____
3 get a train? _____
4 have dinner? _____
5 see a film? _____

6 English sounds Match the pictures and groups 1 to 6. Underline the sound.

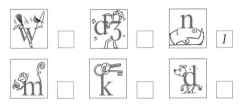

1 fu<u>nn</u>y dow<u>n</u> mid<u>n</u>ight twe<u>n</u>ty ca<u>n</u>'t
2 quick walk once twelve quiet
3 married date record yesterday cold
4 question book case thanks next
5 age orange manager juice change
6 tomorrow summer home small woman

7 📖 English sounds: Vowels *p.142*

Study tip

■ **Remember words in 'families'.**

a Write word groups in your vocabulary file.

	Food	Rooms	Colours
○	banana	hall	white
	pizza	bathroom	red

b Make word maps.

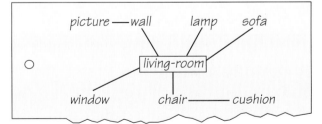

Try it
■ Make a word map for 'restaurant'.

Grammar file 6

1 Object pronouns

I	me	Listen to me.
you	you	I love you.
he	him	She hates him.
she	her	This is Jane. I work with her.
it	it	Do you like it?
we	us	Please give us more money.
you	you	See you tomorrow!
they	them	What do you think of them?

☐ There are eight object pronouns: *me, you*, etc.
☐ Put the object pronoun after the verb / verb + preposition. I hate **you**. NOT ~~I you hate.~~

2 *There is / are + a / an / some / any*

Singular

+	There's	a lamp	
−	There isn't	an ashtray	on the table.
?	Is there	a vase	

✓ ✗	Yes, there is. / No, there isn't.

Plural

+	There are	some photos	
−	There aren't	any books	on the table.
?	Are there	any bananas	

✓ ✗	Yes, there are. / No, there aren't.

☐ Use *a / an* + a singular noun.
☐ Use *some* + plural nouns in ⊞ .
☐ Use *any* + plural nouns in ? and − .

3 Verb *be*: past simple

⊞

I / He / She / It	was	at home last night.
We / You / They	were	

−

I (etc.)	wasn't	at work yesterday.
We (etc.)	weren't	

?

Was	I (etc.)	in class yesterday?
Were	you (etc.)	

✓ ✗

Yes,	I (etc.)	was.	No,	I (etc.)	wasn't.
	you (etc.)	were.		you (etc.)	weren't.

Contractions wasn't = was not weren't = were not

☐ There are only two forms: *was* and *were*.
☐ Present to past: *am / is* → *was, are* → *were.*
He **is** at home today. → He **was** at home last night.

Word order in questions

	Verb	Subject	
	Was	he	in bed last night?
Where	were	you	yesterday?

☐ Put the verb before the subject in questions.

4 *There was / were*

Singular

+	There was	a lamp	
−	There wasn't	an ashtray	on the table.
?	Was there	a vase	

✓ ✗	Yes, there was. / No, there wasn't.

Plural

+	There were	some photos	
−	There weren't	any books	on the table.
?	Were there	any bananas	

✓ ✗	Yes, there were. / No, there weren't.

☐ Present to past: *There is / are* → *There was / were.*

▶ Workbook *p.54* Do **Grammar check 6**. ▶ **Progress chart** (Files 5 / 6) *p.2.* ▶ Do **Check your progress** *p.73.*

Check your progress

Grammar   Right ✓ = **1** point

1 Write a, *an*, *the*, or –.

The children go to __–__ school at 9.00.

1 I always have _____ breakfast at home.

2 They always have _____ sandwich at 11.00.

3 We don't often go to _____ theatre.

4 He has _____ shower before he goes to bed.

5 I finish _____ work at 6.00 every day. ⬜5

2 Complete with a preposition of time.

in on at from until before after

I usually get up *at* 6.30 ¹_____ the morning.
I always go jogging ²_____ breakfast and then I go
to work. I work ³_____ 8.30 ⁴_____ 6.00. ⁵_____
work, I go to the gym for an hour. I don't go out
⁶_____ night very often, only ⁷_____ Fridays. I
often go away ⁸_____ weekends. I usually go on
holiday twice a year: once ⁹_____ Christmas and
again ¹⁰_____ the summer. ⬜10

3 Adverbs. Write correct sentences.

beach never the I to go. *I never go to the beach.*

1 home they get six o'clock usually at

2 go you restaurant often a do how to?

3 time you usually do dinner what have?

4 go we twice about month the cinema to a

5 late always is she ⬜5

4 Complete with an object pronoun.

me ~~you~~ him her us them

I love *you.*

1 I often call _____ but he's never at home.

2 I love Cindy and I think she loves _____.

3 Our children have lunch with _____ every
weekend.

4 I never eat onions. I don't like _____.

5 Do you know Anna? No, I don't know _____. ⬜5

5 Write in the past simple.

I'm tired today. (yesterday) *I was tired yesterday.*

1 Are you at home? (last night)

2 There's a postcard for you. (this morning)

3 Is your brother in Istanbul? (last weekend)

4 She isn't in class. (last Thursday)

5 They aren't at work. (yesterday morning) ⬜5

6 Write the questions.

she there last was night? *Was she there last night?*

1 bedroom your is phone in there a?

2 where you yesterday were?

3 you why like don't Pierre?

4 table letters on there any were the?

5 flat rooms in how there many the are? ⬜5

7 Answer the questions with *because*.

Why did you go to that shop? *Because it's near.*

~~near~~ important expensive hot boring difficult

1 Why don't you like pop music?

2 Why can't you do the exercise?

3 Why don't you get a taxi to work?

4 Why don't you close the window?

5 Why do you want to learn English? ⬜5

Total ⬜ 40

Fluency

1 In English, can you …?   Yes ✓

tell a partner about your typical day. ⬜

describe your living-room. ⬜

say where you were yesterday. ⬜

2 What do you say?

Go to a .

Buy a 🎫 .

Listen to the teacher

1 Write six sentences from the **Travel phrasebook**.

2 Answer the teacher's questions.

Smoking damages your wealth

> *Did she have a cigarette?*
> *No, she didn't.*

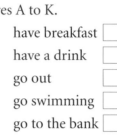

1 Match the phrases and pictures A to K.

go to the gym	H	have breakfast	
go to the hairdresser's		have a drink	
(not) have a cigarette		go out	
have lunch		go swimming	
(not) go to work		go to the bank	
go shopping			

2 Read the text. What happens if Clare or Sarah has a cigarette?

The Devane sisters, Clare and Sarah, inherit $1 million from their aunt – but they only get the money if they stop smoking. If one sister has a cigarette, all the money goes to the other. Clare Devane pays a private detective, Richard Marlow, to follow Sarah …

CLARE Well, Mr Marlow. Did you *follow* Sarah last Friday?

MARLOW Yes, I did.

CLARE Where did she _____, Mr Marlow?

MARLOW Hey, call me Dick.

CLARE Just answer my questions, Marlow.

MARLOW OK, Ms Devane, relax. She went out at about 8.00 a.m. She didn't _____ to work. First she went swimming. Then she had breakfast in a café. After that she –

CLARE But did she _____ a cigarette?

7
A

3 **a** ° 1 ° Listen. Answer the questions.

1 Did Marlow follow Sarah last Friday?
2 Did Sarah go to work last Friday?
3 Did she have a cigarette?

b Complete the dialogue. Listen and check.

GRAMMAR FOCUS

Past simple: *go* / *have*

● Look at the dialogue. Complete the chart.

Present simple	Past simple	
go		
+ I go	→ I went	swimming.
− I don't go	→ I _____ go	
? Do I go	→ _____ I go	to work?
✓✗ Yes, I do. / No, I don't.	→ Yes, I did. / No, I _____.	

have		
+ She has	→ She _____	breakfast.
− She doesn't have	→ She _____ have	
? Does she have	→ _____ she have	a cigarette?
✓✗ Yes, she does. / No, she doesn't.	→ Yes, she _____. / No, she didn't.	

Contraction	_____ = did not

● The past simple form is the same for *I, you* (s.), *he, she, it, we, you* (pl.), and *they*.

PRACTICE

Write past simple sentences.

1 Do they go shopping on Saturdays? (last Saturday)
   Did they go shopping last Saturday?
2 Does she have lunch at one o'clock? (yesterday)
3 He has a drink in a café. (this morning)
4 She doesn't go to the gym on Mondays. (last Monday)
5 I go to the hairdresser's every month. (last month)

4 **a** ° 2 ° Listen. Number pictures A to K in order.

b ° 3 ° Listen to the rest of the dialogue.

1 Did Sarah have a cigarette last Friday?
2 What do you think happens next?

PRONUNCIATION

° 4 ° Listen and repeat.

1 Did you go skiing last weekend?
2 Did you go to the post office?
3 Did you have lunch in a café?
4 Did you watch TV last night?

5 **a** Ask a partner with pictures A to K. Tick ✓ or cross ✗ the pictures for each answer.

A Did you go out yesterday?
B Yes, I did. / No, I didn't. Did you …?

b Swap partners. Say what your first partner did yesterday.
Carlo went out at nine o'clock. He didn't …

6 **a** Write about Sarah's day.
First she … Then she … After that she …

b 🖊 *Have, Go, Get* p.141 *Did you … last weekend?*
Ask a partner.

Saturday night fever?

Did you go out last night?
No, I didn't. I stayed in.

A *stay*   in
B *get*   a taxi
C _____   to bed early / late
D _____   TV
E _____   a film
F _____   for an exam
G _____   to a disco
H _____   some friends
I _____   some flowers
J _____   dinner in a restaurant
K _____   cards
L _____   a meal
M _____   a book

7

B

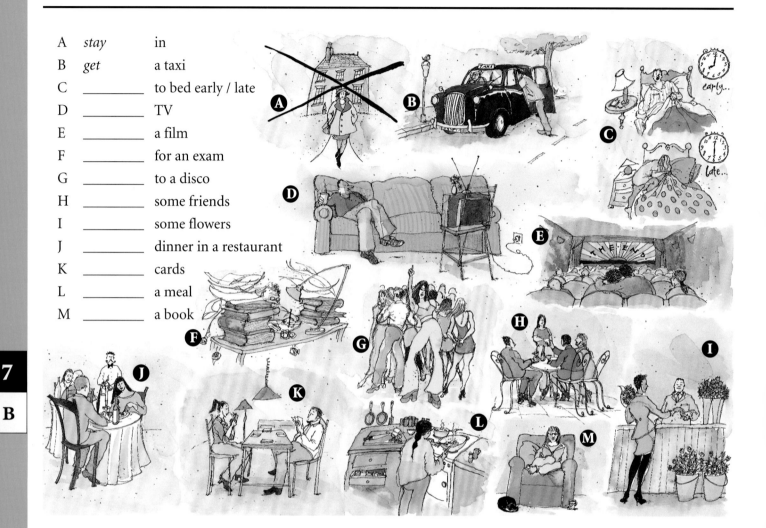

1 I stayed in last Saturday night. I didn't do *anything* special. I cooked a curry for my wife, Anna. _____ the children went to bed, we played cards. _____ we watched TV. Later I read a little, and we _____ a cup of herbal tea. We went to bed early _____ we were both tired. ☐

3 Last Saturday was my sister's birthday. In the afternoon I bought her some flowers. Then I walked to her house about 6.00. All the family were there. We had dinner in a really good restaurant. Then we went to a blues club. We talked and danced, and had a great time. I got a taxi home, and didn't go to bed until 3.30 in the morning. ☐

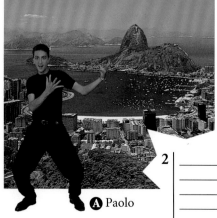

A Paolo

B Ronnie

2 _____ Saturday I studied biology all afternoon for an exam _____ Monday. In the evening I met some friends and we _____ to the beach. Then we had a pizza and saw a film. It _____ awful! My friends went to a disco, but I didn't go. I went _____ to study. I hate exams. ☐

C Sylvie

1 Write verbs for pictures A to M.

2 **a** *Weekend* magazine interviewed Ronnie, Paolo, and Sylvie about last Saturday. Guess what they did. Match each text to a person A to C.

b ° 5 ° Listen and check.

c Listen again. Complete texts 1 and 2.

d ° 6 ° Listen to text 3. Find six mistakes.

GRAMMAR FOCUS

Past simple: regular / irregular verbs

- (Circle) the past simple verbs in the texts.

- Write two letters.
  Past simple regular verbs end in _ _.

PRACTICE

Complete the charts.

Regular verbs	
Infinitive	**Past simple**
cook	*cooked*
dance	_____
talk	_____
walk	_____
watch	_____
play	_____
stay	_____
study	_____

Irregular verbs	
Infinitive	**Past simple**
do	*did*
_____	had
read	_____ /red/
_____	went
get	_____
_____	met
buy	_____ /bɔːt/
_____	saw /sɔː/

PRONUNCIATION

° 7 ° Listen. Repeat the verbs in the grammar chart.

cook   cooked

3 Write questions 6 and 7. Guess. Ask the class.

1 *Did you have dinner at home last Saturday?*

Last Saturday		
How many people ...	**My guess**	**Real number**
1 had dinner at home?	_____	_____
2 studied or worked?	_____	_____
3 saw a good film?	_____	_____
4 spoke English?	_____	_____
5 went away?	_____	_____
6 _____	_____	_____
7 _____	_____	_____

4 **a** ° 8 ° Sophie phones Mona. Listen. Where did Mona go this weekend?

b Listen again. Tick ✓ the questions they ask on the chart.

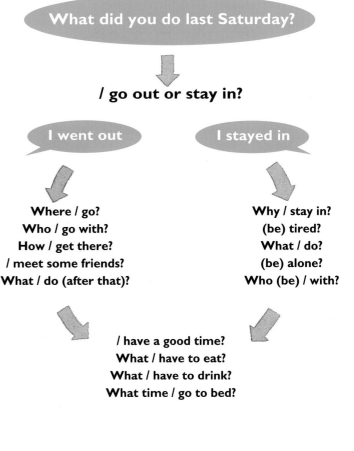

What did you do last Saturday?

/ go out or stay in?

I went out

I stayed in

Where / go?
Who / go with?
How / get there?
/ meet some friends?
What / do (after that)?

Why / stay in?
(be) tired?
What / do?
(be) alone?
Who (be) / with?

/ have a good time?
What / have to eat?
What / have to drink?
What time / go to bed?

c Make questions from the chart. Interview a partner.

7

B

On 14th February

1 **a** Match the words and pictures A to F.

cheque **F**   fax [ ]   boarding card [ ]

newspaper [ ]   receipt [ ]   train ticket [ ]

b ⚬**9**⚬ Listen. Number the pictures in the right order.

2 **a** Use past simple verbs. Write six sentences about Mike.

1 *He bought a newspaper.*

b Look at the pictures. Find three ways to write the date.

3 ○10○ Complete the months. Listen and check. Underline the stress.

-ember (x 3)   -y   -e   -ober   -ch   -ust
-uary   -ruary   -il   -ly

Jan*uary*	Feb_____	Mar_____
Apr_____	Ma_____	Jun_____
Ju_____	Aug_____	Sept_____
Oct_____	Nov_____	Dec_____

4 🖋 Time C *p.136*

PRONUNCIATION

a ○11○

third   fourth   eighth   month
Thursday   theatre

b ○12○ Listen. Repeat the ordinal numbers.

2nd   5th   12th   15th   20th
21st   23rd   30th   31st

c ○13○ Listen and repeat.
/ð/ /θ/   /ð/ /θ/   /θ/ /ð/ /θ/   /θ/
the third   the thirteenth   the thirtieth
/ð/   /θ/ /ð/   /θ/ /ð/   /θ/
the fourth   the fourteenth   the fortieth

5 ○14○ Listen. Write the dates.

1 a radio programme	*28th June*
2 an answerphone	_____
3 a travel agency	_____
4 a ticket agency	_____
5 a bank	_____

When were you born?	I was born	in 1953. on 11th June.
Where were you born?	I was born	in Fiesole, near Florence.
Where did he die?	He died	in Rome.

GRAMMAR FOCUS

Dates

Write	Say
31st December 1999	the thirty-first of December nineteen ninety-nine
January 1st 2000	January the first two thousand

PRACTICE

a Say these.
1 1066   1492   1984   2001
2 14th July   20th August   1/5/94   29.11.89   3rd Sept 2011
3 Henry VIII   Elizabeth II   21C.

b Practise in pairs.
1 Friday 13th February 1333.
2 On Thursday 3rd it's my brother's 35th birthday.
3 They live in the fifth flat on the fourth floor.

c Survey. When's your birthday? Find a student with (nearly) the same birthday as you.

6 Play *Who was I?* Ask the teacher ten questions.

❶ I was born on a train in Siberia in 1938. I died in Paris on 3rd January 1992.

❷ I was born on May 26 1907 and died on June 12 1979. My real name was Marion Morrisson.

Were you …?
European   born in Berlin   a film star good-looking   married   tall

7 Survey. Ask four students.
1 Where were you born?
2 Were you born in hospital?
3 What time were you born?

Yesterday

She typed a letter.

1 Read the newspaper article and answer.

1 What do they do?
2 Did she take a lot of things with her?
3 Why did she leave?
4 Where did she go?

FIND MY WIFE FOR £10,000

● John Harris, a thirty-year-old businessman, yesterday offered £10,000 for information to help him find his wife. Terri, a twenty-seven-year-old journalist, disappeared last week. He said, 'My wife has only a small case and her passport. I don't know why she left or where she went.'

Dear John,

I'm sorry, but

Yesterday was

Please don't

Goodbye.

Terri

John

7

D

A On 3rd March, Terri Harris ...

D After that

G After

B Then

E

H 6 hours ...

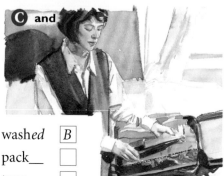

C and

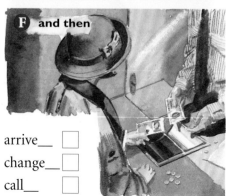

F and then

I After that

And then she disappeared ...

washed [B]
pack__
type__

arrive__
change__
call__

rent__
land__
wait__

80

2 **a** Look at the verbs under the picture story. Complete them in the past simple. Match the verbs and pictures A to I.

b Complete the text.

On 3rd March, Terri Harris *typed* a letter. Then she _____ her hair and _____ a case. After that she _____ a taxi. She _____ at the airport, and then she _____ some money. After the plane _____ she _____ for six hours. After that she _____ a car. And then she disappeared …

c ⁰15° Listen and check.

3 Why is the story in three columns?

PRONUNCIATION

Past simple: regular verbs

There are three ways to pronounce -ed.

/t/	/d/	/ɪd/
washed	called	waited

a ⁰16° Look at the pictures. Listen and repeat.

b ⁰17° Listen. Write /t/, /d/, or /ɪd/.

1 She lived in a small flat.   /d/
2 She wanted to go away.   / ___ /
3 She booked a plane ticket.   / ___ /
4 She travelled alone.   / ___ /

c ⁰18° Listen. Say 'past' or 'present'.

1 I need a new car. = *present*

4 Look at the pictures. Tell a partner the story.

5 **a** With the teacher, list ten regular and ten irregular verbs.

b In groups, say things you did / didn't do this morning.
I listened to the radio.

6 **a** ⁰19° 🎵 Listen to *Yesterday*. Complete the song.

~~away~~   be   me   play   say   stay   yesterday (x 3)

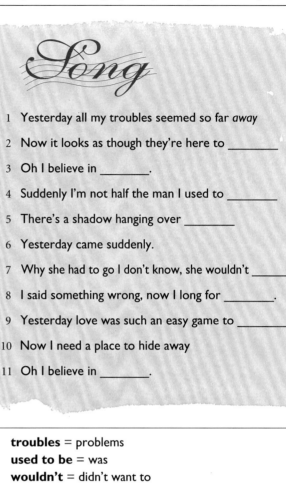

Song

1 Yesterday all my troubles seemed so far *away*
2 Now it looks as though they're here to _____
3 Oh I believe in _____.
4 Suddenly I'm not half the man I used to _____
5 There's a shadow hanging over _____
6 Yesterday came suddenly.
7 Why she had to go I don't know, she wouldn't _____
8 I said something wrong, now I long for _____.
9 Yesterday love was such an easy game to _____
10 Now I need a place to hide away
11 Oh I believe in _____.

troubles = problems
used to be = was
wouldn't = didn't want to
long for = want something very much
hide = go where people can't find you

b What does the song mean? Tick ✓ 1 or 2.

1 ☐ Yesterday life was great. Then she left me. Now I feel awful.

2 ☐ Yesterday life was awful. So I left her. Now I feel great.

7

D

White Death

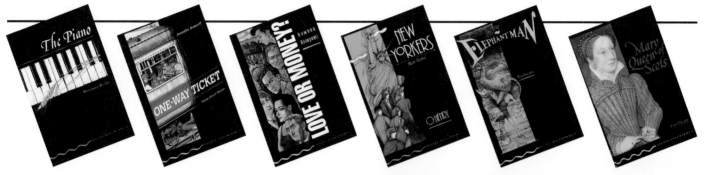

Reading helps you learn English more quickly.
Easy Readers can help you:

1 remember grammar and vocabulary.
2 learn new vocabulary.
3 enjoy reading in English.

Tip 1

Before you read, look at the cover.

1 **a** Look at the title and pictures. What kind of story
is it? Does it interest you?

b Read the back cover. Can you understand the
story? What's it about? Does it interest you?

c What's *White Death*?

WHITE DEATH

Sarah Harland is nineteen and she's in prison. At
the airport they find h… in her bag. So now she is
waiting to go to court. If the court decides that it
was her h…, then she must die.

She says she did not do it. But if she did not, who
did? Only two people can help Sarah: her mother
and an old boyfriend who does not love her now.
Can they find the criminal before it is too late?

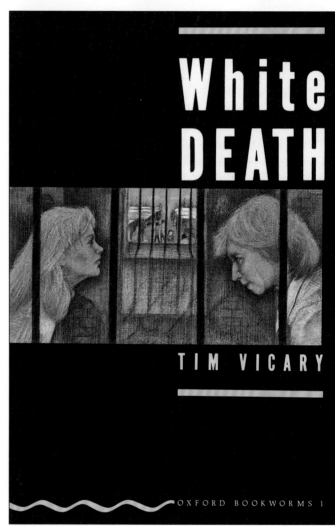

Tip 2

When you read, stop and ask yourself questions.

2 Read **Extract 1** once. Answer the questions.

1 What do you know about the woman?
2 Which country is she in?
3 What does she want to do?

Tip 3

When you can't understand a new word, don't always
use a dictionary. Read the sentence. Look at the
spelling. Try to guess the meaning.

3 **a** Read **Extract 1** again. Are the words in *italics*
nouns, adjectives, or verbs?

b Guess the meaning of the words.

Extract 1

The woman *stood* in front of the *prison.* The woman was very *hot,* and she did not like the *noise* from all the cars in the road. She was an English woman and she did not like hot countries
5 or a lot of noise. She was tall, about fifty years old, with blue eyes and a long *face.* Her face was red, and she looked tired and *angry.* She *knocked* at the door of the prison. For a long time nothing happened. Then a little window opened in the
10 door, and a man looked out at her.

Extract 2

'Yes? What do you want?'
'I want to see my daughter. It's very important.'
'Name?'
'Anne Harland.'
15 'Wait a minute.'
After twenty minutes the door opened. 'Come with *me,*' the man said. She walked for a long time, past hundreds of doors. Then the man opened one of *them.* 'In here,' he said. 'You can
20 have ten minutes.' Anne Harland walked into the room and the man went in after *her.* He closed the door behind *him.* There was a table in the room, and two chairs. On one of the chairs sat her daughter. *She* was a tall girl, about nineteen
25 years old, with big blue eyes.
'Mother!' she said. 'I'm so happy to see *you.*'

Extract 3

'Sarah, what happened?' she said. 'When did they bring you to this prison?'
'Last week, I think. Yes, last week. At the airport,
30 when we arrived . . . The police stopped us, and looked in our bags. They said there were drugs in my bag. Then they brought me here.'
'I see. Where were the drugs, then? Where did they find them?'
35 'Didn't they tell you?' Sarah looked up, and there was a smile on her face, but it was not a happy smile. 'The drugs were in a tube of toothpaste.'
'And you didn't know about it?'
'No, mother, of course not. Do you think I clean
40 my teeth with heroin?'

Tip 4

When you can't guess a word, either a) don't worry about it – read on, or b) use the glossary, or a dictionary.

4 Read **Extract 2**. Who are the woman, the man, and the girl?

Tip 5

Look carefully at pronouns. What do they mean? For example, look at *me* (line 17): *me* = the man.

5 What do the other pronouns in *italics* mean?

Tip 6

Try to read quickly.

6 Read **Extract 3** in one minute. Answer the questions.
   1 When and where did the police arrest Sarah?
   2 Was she alone?
   3 What did the police find in her toothpaste?
   4 How does the story end? Guess. Ask the teacher.

Tip 7

Use what you read to help you a) revise, and b) learn new words.

7 Choose five words from the story to remember. Write them in your vocabulary list.

7

court *n.* = a place where judges and lawyers work
death *n.* = end of life
toothpaste *n.* = stuff for cleaning your teeth
brought *v.* = bring (past simple)
sat *v.* = sit (past simple)
stood *v.* = stand (past simple)

Directions

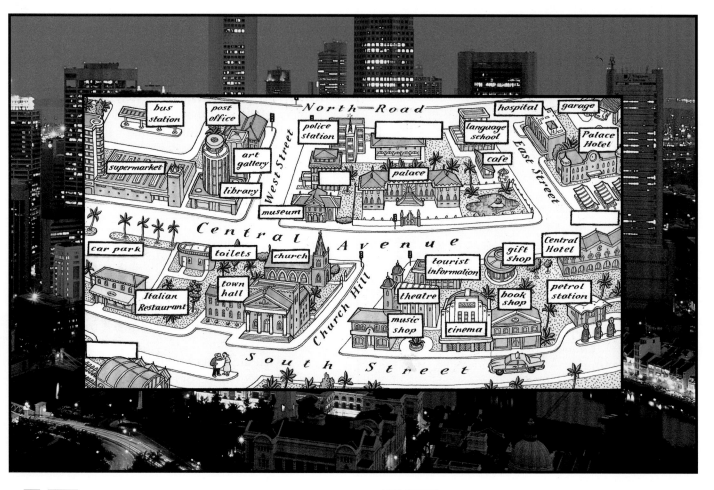

1 **a** ° 21 °   Listen. Point to the right place.

b Practise in pairs.

A It's in West Street, opposite the police station.
B The post office. It's …

2 **a** ° 22 °   Listen. Complete the map.

b Practise in pairs.

A Is there a garage near here?
B Yes, there's one in North Road, next to the hospital.

❶ opposite   **❷ on the corner**

3 **a** Match the words and pictures A to D.

Turn left.	*C*
Turn right at the traffic lights.	☐
Go straight on.	☐
Go past the palace.	☐

b ° 23 °   Listen to a tourist in a taxi. Where does she go?

c Role-play *Taxi!* Ask the teacher.

4 **a** ° 24 °   Listen. How do you get to the station?

b Listen again. Complete the questions.

Could you *tell* me the way to the _____?
Could you _____ that again, please?
Could you _____ more slowly, please?
Could you _____ me on the map?

c Listen and repeat.

d You're in South Street. Practise directions.

A Excuse me. Could you tell me the way to …?
B Yes, of course. Go …

5 📖 **Travel phrasebook 7** *p.131*

Game

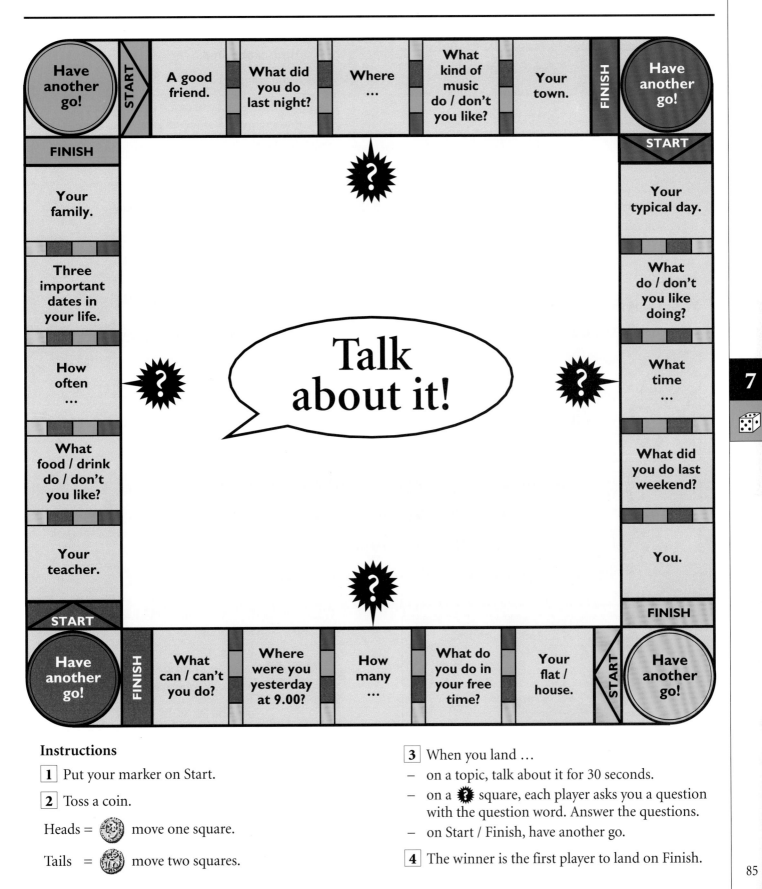

Instructions

1. Put your marker on Start.

2. Toss a coin.

Heads = move one square.

Tails = move two squares.

3. When you land …
   - on a topic, talk about it for 30 seconds.
   - on a **?** square, each player asks you a question with the question word. Answer the questions.
   - on Start / Finish, have another go.

4. The winner is the first player to land on Finish.

The good, the bad, and the holiday

1 **a** Number the time expressions 1st to 10th.

last November	☐	six months ago	☐
a month ago	☐	three weeks ago	☐
a year ago	☐	two hours ago	☐
last weekend	☐	three days ago	☐
last Monday	☐	in 1973	*1st*

b Play *True or false*. Write six sentences, some true ✓, some false ✗. Swap. Guess ✓ or ✗ in pairs. *I got married six months ago.*

2 **a** ⟨ 25 ⟩ Listen. Number the three pictures you hear 1 to 3.

When was the last time you …?

b Ask a partner with pictures A to E. Ask more questions, too.

A When was the last time you cried at the cinema?
B (About) six months ago. / A long time ago. / Last night.
A What film did you see?

Past time expressions
Where did you go last year?
Last year / Three months ago I went to France. I went to France last year / three months ago. NOT ~~the last year~~

3 Put the words in the right order.

1 home ago minutes five arrived She.
   She arrived home five minutes ago.
2 I the to week last dentist's went.
3 drove He Russia to ago years two.
4 Tuesday night you did go Where last?
5 came Britain January to They last.

4 **a** What do you like doing on holiday? Choose your top three.

sunbathing	☐
visiting historical places	☐
going to museums	☐
eating in restaurants	☐
going shopping	☐
going to the mountains	☐
taking photos	☐
reading good books	☐

b Read the letter from *Holiday* magazine. Complete the questions.

Who?   When?   How long?   How?
Where?   ~~Why?~~   What

1	*Why* did she go to France?	For a holiday.
2	_____ did she go?	Three months ago.
3	_____ did she go with?	Her husband.
4	_____ did they get there?	By boat and car.
5	_____ did they stay?	In small hotels.
6	_____ did they stay?	For two weeks.
7	_____ did they do?	They sunbathed and read.

The good, the bad and the holiday

Last month in *Holiday* magazine, we asked readers to write and tell us about their holidays – good or bad. Here is the best letter.

Dear *Holiday* magazine,

Three months ago I went on holiday to the south of France with my husband. We went by boat and car. We were there for two weeks and we stayed in small hotels. We had a very good time. We sunbathed and read books. We went to the beach every day. We visited a lot of historical places. The weather was lovely and the food in France was wonderful. But …

5 **a** What happens next: something good, or something bad?

b ○26○ Listen. Number the pictures 1 to 4.

c Put the story in the right order 1 to 4.

But on the last day our car broke down. We didn't speak French and we needed to get to Boulogne to get the boat to England. Luckily, we met another Englishman, Simon Pike. He was very friendly. He had a car and he took us to Paris to get the train to Boulogne. **1**

We ran to platform 7 and got on the train. We said goodbye and thank you to Simon. 'You're welcome,' he said. 'Have a good trip!' The train left, and we started to talk to an Italian tourist. ☐

'What time do we arrive in Boulogne?' we asked. 'Boulogne?' he said. 'I think you have a problem. This train goes to … ☐

When we arrived at the station, Simon said, 'Don't worry. I speak a little French.' He ran to the ticket office and bought us two tickets. He asked a guard in French, 'Excuse me! Which platform for Boulogne?' 'Platform 7,' said the guard, 'but hurry! It leaves in two minutes.' ☐

6 **a** Ask questions about a partner's last holiday. *Where did you go? Who did you …?*

b Write to *Holiday* magazine about one of your holidays, good or bad! *Last (summer) I / we …*

7 Do the competition.

And finally in *Holiday* magazine this month, another
★ **'Fun with the famous' competition,** ★
also about France.

WHEN Hollywood stars Tom Cruise and Nicole Kidman visited Paris for the first time, they spent only one day in that beautiful and historical city. Guess what they did. Write three things on a postcard.

Send it to:
Holiday magazine,
Manchester M69 4VP.

Vocabulary file 7

1 Verbs Complete the phrases.

1 t a k e a photo / an aspirin
2 _ a _ e lunch / a cup of coffee
3 w _ _ t for an hour / for a bus
4 _ t _ y in / for two weeks
5 _ u _ flowers / a new car
6 b _ o _ a ticket / a holiday
7 _ e e _ some friends / for the first time

2 Puzzle Write the next word(s).

1 February April *June*
2 last week this week _____
3 tomorrow today _____
4 tenth twentieth _____
5 once twice _____

3 Questions Complete and answer.

| How often   Which   ~~When~~ |
| What kind of   How long   Why |

1 *When* do you go on holiday?
2 _____ did you stay in Paris?
3 _____ don't you like the winter?
4 _____ music do you like?
5 _____ do you go to the cinema?
6 _____ do you prefer: spring or autumn?

4 Prepositions Complete with for on opposite past .

1 The cinema is _____ the museum.
2 They lived in Athens _____ fifteen years.
3 I was born _____ 25th March 1977.
4 Go _____ the post office.

5 English sounds Underline the right sounds. Say the sentences.

1 Beautiful young university students.
2 Terry's very sorry. The restaurant was terrible.
3 The English like dogs, golf, and gardens.
4 Five fat friends in a photo.
5 Horrible Henry's hot, happy, and hungry.
6 A lovely video of Vladivostok.

6 📖 **House** *p.138* Play *Hide and find*.

A 'Hide' a coin. 🪙 B Guess. Swap.
B Is it in the …? / next to the …? / under the …?, etc.
A Yes, it is. / No, it isn't.

Study tip

■ **Keep a record of irregular verbs.**

a Write Irregular (Irr) next to verbs with an irregular past simple form.

○
> call
> do (Irr) = did
> change
> come (Irr) = came
> read (Irr) = read /red/

b Write verbs in two columns.

Regular	Irregular
call – called	come – came

○

c Use a dictionary.

go /gəʊ/ v. (past tense *went* /went /)

went /went/ past tense of v. *go*

Try it!

📖 **Irregular verbs** *p.144*

■ Find the infinitive of these verbs.
   found spoke thought

■ Find the past simple of these verbs.
   can give make

■ Test yourself with 📖 **Irregular verbs**. Look at the past simple. Remember the infinitive.

Grammar file 7

1 Present to past

	Present simple			Past simple		
+	I / You / We / They He / She / It	work works	for IBM.	I (etc.)	worked	for IBM.
–	I (etc.) He (etc.)	don't work doesn't			didn't work	
?	Do you (etc.)	work		Did you (etc.)	work	
	What time	does	the film finish?	What time	did	the film finish?

☐ The past simple is the same for all personal pronouns (*I* / *he*, etc.).　　☐ Use *did* in ? and *didn't* in – .

2 Past simple

+ Regular verbs

Present		Past		Spelling
I	watch play	I	watched played	+ ed
	live smoke		lived smoked	+ d
	stop		stopped	1 vowel + 1 consonant → double consonant
	study		studied	consonant + y → ied

Pronunciation

voiced (e.g. play)	/d/	played　lived　studied
unvoiced (e.g. watch)	/t/	watched　kissed　stopped
ending /t/ and /d/ (e.g. want / need)	/ɪd/	wanted　needed　painted

+ Irregular verbs

Present	Past
I go I have I meet I see	I went I had I met I saw

☐ Verbs are only irregular in **+** .

✎ **Irregular verbs** *p.144*

– Regular and irregular verbs

I (etc.)	didn't	see a film arrive	yesterday.

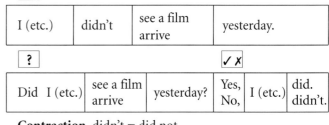

?				**✓ ✗**		
Did I (etc.)	see a film arrive	yesterday?	Yes, No,	I (etc.)	did. didn't.

Contraction didn't = did not

☐ Use *didn't* + infinitive in negatives.
　NOT ~~I didn't saw a film.~~
☐ Use *did* + infinitive in questions.
　NOT ~~Did you saw …?~~

Word order in questions

Question	**A**uxiliary	**S**ubject	**I**nfinitive	
	Did	you	go out	last night?
Who	did	they	go	with?
What	did	Pam	do?	

☐ Remember: word order = A S I and Q A S I
▶ **Present simple** *p.39*

3 Past time expressions

He went to the USA	yesterday (afternoon). this morning, etc. last night / week / month / year. in 1989. two years ago.

☐ Don't use *the*. NOT ~~the last year~~
☐ Time expressions can go at the beginning or end of a sentence.

▶ Workbook *p.55* Do **Grammar check 7**.

Watching you watching me

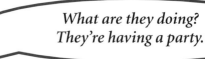

What are they doing?
They're having a party.

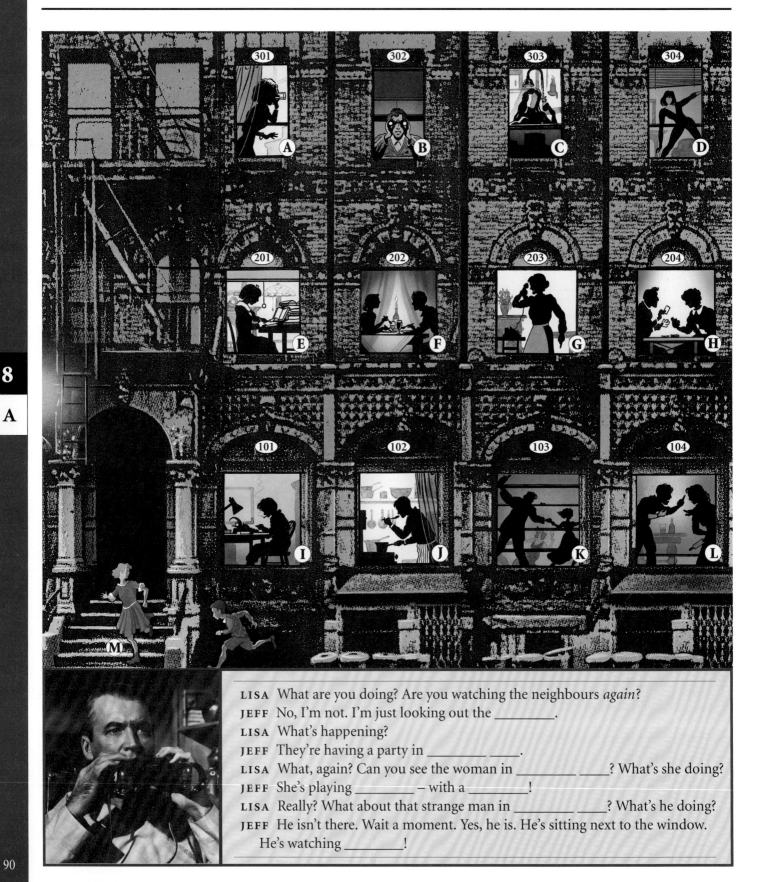

8

A

LISA What are you doing? Are you watching the neighbours *again*?

JEFF No, I'm not. I'm just looking out the _____.

LISA What's happening?

JEFF They're having a party in _____ ____.

LISA What, again? Can you see the woman in _____ ____? What's she doing?

JEFF She's playing _____ – with a _____!

LISA Really? What about that strange man in _____ ____? What's he doing?

JEFF He isn't there. Wait a moment. Yes, he is. He's sitting next to the window.
He's watching _____!

Rear Window (Alfred Hitchcock, 1954, US) James Stewart, Grace Kelly. 112 min. PG Video CIC £9.99 VHS VHR1126
Jeff (James Stewart) is a photographer in New York. He's got a broken leg and can't leave his flat. So he starts watching his neighbours.

1 Write verbs / phrases for pictures A to M.

A *listen to the neighbours*

2 **a** ° **1** ° Lisa (Jeff's girlfriend, played by Grace Kelly) phones. Listen. Which flats do they talk about?

b Listen again. Complete the dialogue.

PRONUNCIATION

° **2** ° Listen. Copy the intonation.

1 *What* are you *doing*?

GRAMMAR FOCUS

Present continuous

● Use *be* + (verb)-*ing*.

I'm You're (etc.)	singing in the rain.

● Complete the chart.

+	−
She's **having** a shower.	_____
_____	He **isn't cooking** a meal.
They're **playing** cards.	_____

?	✓ ✗
_____	Yes, she is.
_____	No, _____.
Are they **playing** cards?	Yes, _____.

PRACTICE

a Complete the chart.

1		2		3	
study	*studying*	have	*having*	sit	*sitting*
watch	_____	smoke	_____	run	_____
look	_____	type	_____		

b What's the -*ing* form of these verbs?

wash   live   stop   clean   make   go   cry   get

3 **a** Look at pictures A to M. What are they doing?

A *She's listening to the neighbours.*

b Test a partner. Point and ask.

A   What's she doing?
B   She's having a shower. What are they doing?

4 **a** ° **3** ° Listen. What are they doing?

b 🖊 **Jobs** *p.137* **A** Choose a person. Say 'man' or 'woman'. **B** Ask questions. Guess.
Is he (playing football)?

5 What are your neighbours / family / friends (probably) doing now?
My sister's (probably) studying.

6 **a** Read the rest of the film review.

A classic Hitchcock film. The camera never leaves Jeff's flat. Hitchcock shows us the sad 'silent film' of other peoples' lives. **Brilliant.** ★★★★★

b Do you like watching other people? Where?
I like watching people at supermarkets, on planes …

c Do you watch your neighbours?

7 Play *Don't say a word* in teams. Ask the teacher.

8

A

Fashion

> *What's she wearing?*
> *A long, black skirt.*

belt /belt/ ☐
boots /buːts/ ☐
coat /kəʊt/ ☐
dress /dres/ ☐
glasses /ˈglɑːsɪz/ ☐
hat /hæt/ ☐
jacket /ˈdʒækɪt/ ☐
jeans /dʒiːnz/ ☐
shirt /ʃɜːt/ ☐
shoes /ʃuːz/ ☐
skirt /skɜːt/ ☐
socks /sɒks/ ☐
suit /suːt/ ☐
sweater /ˈswetə/ ☐
T-shirt /ˈtiːʃɜːt/ ☐
tie /taɪ/ ☐ *F*
trainers /ˈtreɪnəz/ ☐
trousers /ˈtraʊzəz/ ☐

sw**ea**ter
sweater /ˈswetə/ *n.*   = word stress **V**

light-blue │ dark blue

> Tonight, _____'s wearing a long,
> light-brown coat, a blue and green
> sweater, and dark red trousers.
> She isn't wearing any shoes or
> socks, and she's carrying some
> flowers. This fashion is from the
> 19___s.

8
B

92

1 **a** Read and complete the commentator's words.

  b ◦4◦ Listen and check. Match five clothes words with pictures A to E.

2 **a** Match the other clothes with pictures F to R.

  b ◦5◦ Look at the phonetics. Pronounce each word. Listen and check.

3 **a** Look at model 2. Write the clothes he's wearing in the right column.

Singular	Plural
He's wearing a … *blue jacket*	He's wearing … *red trousers*

b **A** Describe a model. Don't say he or she. **B** Guess. Swap.

This model's wearing (a / an) …

4 ⚬ **6** ⚬ Listen to the fashion show. Who's she describing?

5 Do the questionnaire in groups.

Are **you** interested in clothes?

I What do you usually wear at …
  a work / school?
  b home?
  c a wedding?

2 How often do you …
  d buy new clothes?

once a month	☐
every six months	☐
hardly ever	☐

  e read fashion magazines?

every month	☐
sometimes	☐
never	☐

  f look at clothes in shops?

very often	☐
sometimes	☐
hardly ever	☐

3 **g** What's the teacher wearing?
  h Are you wearing fashionable clothes now?
  i Is anybody in the class wearing very fashionable clothes?

4 **j** What's in fashion now?
  k Are you in fashion?

GRAMMAR FOCUS

Present simple or continuous?

> What do you wear every day? = present simple
> What are you wearing now? = present continuous

● Write 'simple' or 'continuous'.

Use the present _____ for what's happening now.

Use the present _____ for what happens every day / week, etc.

● Look at the questionnaire. Which tenses are they? Why?

PRACTICE

a Write *now* or *every day*.

1 She's a typist. She types letters _____.
2 It's 10.00. She's typing a letter _____.
3 I wear a tie to work _____.
4 I'm not wearing a tie _____, because it's Saturday.

b Write questions.

1 / usually wear perfume (aftershave)?
  Do you usually wear perfume?
2 / wear perfume (aftershave) today?
  Are you wearing perfume today?
3 What newspaper / usually read?
4 What / read now?
5 What / do now?
6 What / do?

6 Play *Fashion show.* **A** Describe somebody in the room. **B** Guess. Swap.

⚬ **7** ⚬

    pink type stop present purple happy

long light black clothes little glasses

Spend, spend, spend

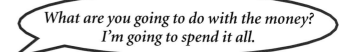

What are you going to do with the money?
I'm going to spend it all.

⚽		⚽	
Chelsea	1	Queen's Park Rangers	2
Liverpool	2	Arsenal	__
Manchester United	__	West Ham	__
Sheffield Wednesday	__	Norwich City	__

Housewife wins millions on pools!

Yesterday, mother-of-four **Vivian Nicholson** won **£2 million** on the football pools. Lucky Vivian, a 24-year-old housewife, said, 'I can't believe it! I'm rich …'

1 Number the time expressions 1st to 8th.

today	1st	next summer	
tonight		tomorrow night	
next month		tomorrow morning	
next year		next Thursday	

2 **a** ° 8 ° Listen. Complete the football results. How does the woman feel?

b Write five questions about her.

~~name~~   married   children   job   age

1 *What's her name?*

c Read the article. Answer the five questions.

3 **a** Match the words and pictures A to F.

buy a big house	B	have a holiday	
put it in the bank		buy a Rolls Royce	
have a party		travel round the world	

b ° 9 ° Listen. What's she going to do? Tick ✓ or cross ✗ the pictures.

c Match the questions and answers below. Listen again and check.

1	Congratulations, Vivian. How do you feel?	d	a	No, I'm not. I can't drive!
2	Are you going to have a party?		b	Yes, I'm going to travel round the world.
3	What's the first thing you're going to buy?		c	I'm going to spend, spend, spend!
4	Are you going to buy a Rolls Royce?		d	Great ! Wonderful! Fantastic!
5	Are you going to have a holiday?		e	Yes, I am – a big party for all my friends.
6	What are you going to do with the money?		f	A big house in the country.

8

C

4 Imagine you're a journalist. Write about her plans.
Mrs Nicholson's got big plans for the future. She says she's going to … She isn't going to …

GRAMMAR FOCUS

Future plans: (*be*) *going to* …

- Use (*be*) *going to* + infinitive.
- Complete the chart.

+	I _____ going to travel round the world.
−	She _____ going to buy a car.
?	_____ you going to have a party?
✓ ✗	Yes, I _____. / No, I _____ not.

PRACTICE

a Put the words in the right order.
1 going you tomorrow tennis to Are play?
  Are you going to play tennis tomorrow?
2 going to Friday a new jacket buy on I'm.
3 tonight What you to are going do?
4 to isn't going study He this evening.
5 they early going to finish work Are today?

b Write six true sentences about your plans, three positive and three negative.
I'm not going to have a holiday this year.

PRONUNCIATION

a ⟨°10°⟩ Listen. Write five sentences.

b Say the sentences quickly. Here, *to* = /tə/.

5 ✏ **Verbs** *p.139 Are you going to … tomorrow?* Ask a partner.

6 a Role-play in fours.

> **A and B**
> You're a couple. You're pools winners. What are you going to do with the money?

> **C and D**
> You're journalists. Write six questions to ask the pools winners. Interview **A** and **B** separately. Do they agree?

b Ask a partner about his / her plans.

Tonight	**Tomorrow**
/ study English?	/ do anything special?
/ go out?	What time / get up?
What / have for dinner?	Where / have lunch?
What / do after dinner?	What / do in the evening?

Next weekend	**Next summer**
/ go away?	/ have a holiday?
/ stay in on Saturday night?	Where / go?

Surprise, surprise!

Surprise, surprise!

One night Eric and Brenda Crow woke up suddenly at three o'clock in the morning. 'I heard a noise,' said Brenda. 'Was it our car?' She looked out of the window, *but* she couldn't see their car. *So* she called the police. 'How are we going to get to work tomorrow?' she asked Eric.

Next morning they got up early *and* ran to the station. They went to work by train. *But when* they got home in the evening they got a nice surprise. Their car was outside their house again! *When* they looked inside they found some red roses and an envelope. Brenda opened the envelope. There was a letter and two tickets for *The Phantom of the Opera* on Friday. She read the letter. It said:

> **I'm very sorry. I took your car because my mother was ill. I had to take her to hospital. I hope you understand. Thank you very much. Have a good time!**
> **Tony**

So on Friday evening Eric and Brenda drove to Manchester. They had dinner in a French restaurant. *After that* they saw the show. They had a really good time. *Then* they went home. They got home at 1.00 in the morning *and* parked outside their house. They were tired and happy. *But when* they opened the front door they got an awful surprise …

1 **a** Look at the pictures. What's happening?
A *They're running.*

b ◦**11**◦ Listen. Number the pictures in order.

c Read the story and check.

d Find and circle the irregular verbs.

2 ◦**12**◦ Guess. What was the awful surprise? Listen. Were you right?

3 ►◄ Question practice PAIR A *p.120* PAIR B *p.123*

4 **a** Story-telling. Look at the pictures. Listen to the story again.

b Write the connectors on the right pictures.

c A Look only at the pictures and connectors. Tell the story. B Listen to A. Help and correct. Swap.

On the phone

Could I speak to Donna Rice ?

JOE I'll call back later.	☐
RECEPTIONIST One moment, please … Sorry, it's engaged. Would you like to hold?	☐
RECEPTIONIST XTC. Good morning. Can I help you?	1st
JOE Yes, OK.	☐
JOE Could I speak to Donna Rice, please?	☐
RECEPTIONIST I'm sorry. It's still engaged.	☐

Is that Joe …?

Donna

8

1 **a** ° 13 ° Listen. Does he speak to Donna?

b Listen again. Number the dialogue in the right order 1st to 6th.

2 **a** ° 14 ° Listen to three more calls. Is this text in the right order?

> First Joe got the wrong number. Then he phoned a fax machine. After that he left a message on Donna's answerphone.

b Listen again. Complete these sentences.

1 I'm _____ . I _____ you've got the _____ number.

2 Please _____ a message _____ the beep.

c Listen again. Take Joe's message.

Messages

Joe H _____ *from* _____ _____
Tel: _____ *Room number* _____

3 **a** ° 15 ° Listen. Complete the message for Donna from Bill.

> I _____ called ___ say Bill _____ _____ .

b Add CAPITAL letters, full stops (.), and question marks (?).

1 couldispeaktomrjoehanseninroom501, please
2 justamoment, please
3 isthatjoehansen
4 hellojoe, thisisdonnarice
5 i'vegotanimportantmessageforyoufrombill

4 Role-play. **A** You're Joe. **B** You're the receptionist, 'wrong number', and Donna.

5 Choose three 'phone phrases'. Write a dialogue.

6 ◫ **Travel phrasebook 8** *p.131*

° 16 ° ♫ *I just called to say I love you*, Stevie Wonder

Contraction I'll = I will

At Tom's Diner

1 In pairs, remember the story in File 7D.
First she typed a letter. Then …

2 Look at the picture. Answer the questions.

1 Which country's Terri in?
   I think she's in … because …
2 Is it morning, afternoon, or evening?
3 What season is it?
4 Is the weather good?
5 What's she wearing?
6 What's she doing?
7 Is she happy?
8 What's she going to do?

3 ⟨°17°⟩ Listen. Number in order 1 to 5.

It's raining.	☐
He's pouring the coffee.	1
She's shaking the umbrella.	☐
They're kissing.	☐
The bells are ringing.	☐

4 a ⟨°18°⟩ 🎵 Listen to *Tom's Diner*.
Complete with the verbs (*-ing* form).

come   kiss   listen   look   pretend
shake   ~~sit~~   think   wait

b Listen and check. Complete the
last line of the song.

5 Look at Terri's bag. What's she going to do?

6 a ►◄ **The end of the story?** A *p.120*
B *p.123* **C** *p.123* Which do you think is true?

b ⟨°19°⟩ Listen and check.

Song

1 I am *sitting* in the morning at the diner on the corner

2 I am _____ at the counter for the man to pour the coffee

3 And he fills it only half-way and before I even argue

4 He is _____ out the window at somebody _____ in.

5 'It is always nice to see you!' says the man behind the counter

6 To the woman who has come in, she is _____ her umbrella

7 And I look the other way as they are _____ their hellos and

8 I'm _____ not to see them and instead I pour the milk.

9 Oh, this rain it will continue through the morning as I'm _____

10 To the bells of the cathedral. I am _____ of your voice

11 And of the midnight picnic once upon a time before the rain began.

12 And I finish up my coffee and it's time to …

Vocabulary file 8

1 Clothes Find the words.

1 toca   *coat*
2 najes   _____
3 krits   _____
4 itus   _____
5 strosh   _____
6 routress _____

2 Verbs Match the verbs and phrases.

do eat find send ~~see~~ spend wear win

1 *see* a film / some friends
2 _____ £2 million / a game
3 _____ an exam / homework
4 _____ a letter / postcards
5 _____ meat / in a restaurant
6 _____ a shirt / new shoes
7 _____ money
8 _____ money / your keys

3 Time expressions Write *next*, *last*, or *ago*.

1 I saw her two days _____.
2 We're going to have a party _____ Saturday.
3 What did you do _____ night?
4 He was born thirty years _____.
5 Where were you _____ night?
6 _____ year I'm going to drive round the USA.

4 Puzzle ⟨Circle⟩ the different word.

1 near under ⟨because⟩ next to
2 go see watch speak
3 morning afternoon evening night
4 March Monday June September
5 bill food phone starter
6 cassette stamp board teacher
7 carefully slower fast happily

5 Prepositions Complete with round inside outside .

1 They parked the car _____ the house.
2 I'm going to travel _____ the world.
3 _____ the envelope they found some tickets.

6 English sounds Match the pictures and sentences 1 to 6. Say the sentences.

1 A piece of pizza, an apple, and a purple, paper cup.
2 Tired teachers wear jackets, shirts, and ties.
3 My mother's brother's father is my mother's father.
4 Ingrid likes reading, running, singing, and sleeping.
5 She washes her shoes in the shower.
6 Cheese sandwiches, chips, and chocolate for lunch.

7 📖 Verbs *p.139* Ask a partner. Swap.

A When was the last time you went on holiday?
B Two weeks ago. / Last June., etc.

Study tip

■ **Learn all the English sounds.**

📖 **English sounds** *p.142* Cover the words. Look at the pictures. Say the words.

Try it!

■ 📖 **English sounds: Consonants** *p.143*
■ Choose and practise five sounds from **English sounds** which are difficult for you.

1 Present continuous

+

I	'm	
You / We / They	're	studying.
He / She / It	's	

−

I	'm not	
You / We / They	aren't	studying.
He / She / It	isn't	

?

Am	I	
Are	you / we / they	studying?
Is	he / she / it	

✓ ✗

Yes,	I am.	No,	I'm not.
	we are.		we aren't.
	she is.		she isn't.

☐ Spelling of *-ing* form.
▶ *like / love / hate* + (verb)-*ing* p.50

Word order in questions

	Verb *be*	Subject	*-ing* form
	Is	he	cleaning the house?
What	are	they	doing?

☐ Put the verb *be* before the subject in questions.

2 Simple or continuous?

Present simple	Present continuous
My sister works in a bank.	Today she's working at home.
I always have breakfast at 7.00.	It's 7.00 now. I'm having breakfast.

☐ Use the present simple for things you do every day / week / year, etc.
☐ Use the present continuous for things you are doing now.

3 Future plans: (*be*) *going to* …

+

I	'm	
You (etc.)	're	going to buy a car.
He (etc.)	's	

−

I	'm not	
You (etc.)	aren't	going to buy a car.
He (etc.)	isn't	

?

Am	I	
Are	you (etc.)	going to buy a car?
Is	he (etc.)	

✓ ✗

Yes,	I am.	No,	I'm not.
	she is.		she isn't.
	we are.		we aren't.

What are you going to do next weekend?
I'm going to (go to) Bucharest next year.

☐ Use (*be*) *going to* + infinitive for future plans.
☐ With the verb *go* you don't need to say *go* twice.

4 Future time expressions

We're going to get married	today / tonight. this morning / afternoon / evening. tomorrow (morning, etc.). next week / month / summer / year.

☐ Time expressions can go at the beginning or end of a sentence.
▶ **Past time expressions** *p.89*

5 *it*

What time is it?   It's 11.30. It's late. It's 12th January. It's Friday. It's my birthday. It's hot today. It rained yesterday.

☐ Use *it* for times, dates, and weather.

8
G

100

▶ Workbook *p.56* Do **Grammar check 8**. ▶ **Progress chart** (Files 7 / 8) *p.3*. ▶ Do **Check your progress** *p.101*.

Check your progress

Grammar   Right ✓ = **1** point

1 Write the questions.

you night work last did? *Did you work last night?*
1 Saturday what they did on night do?
2 studying sister is your English?
3 do weekend to you what going are next?
4 to Lena go did yesterday work?
5 tomorrow to parents come going your are? [ ] 5

2 Write the negatives.

She's playing tennis. *She isn't playing tennis.*
1 I was at work yesterday.
2 They saw a film last night.
3 We're going to buy a new car.
4 I'm living with my parents now.
5 She called me this morning. [ ] 5

3 Complete with the past simple.

study ~~be~~ write leave meet start make be die
go murder be get married

John Lennon *was* born in Liverpool in 1940. He
[1]_____ art at Liverpool College of Art. His
mother [2]_____ in a road accident when he
[3]_____ eighteen. He [4]_____ playing with the
Beatles in 1960 in Hamburg. With Paul McCartney
he [5]_____ hundreds of songs for the Beatles,
including *Help!*, and *All you need is love*. In 1966 he
[6]_____ Yoko Ono, a Japanese artist, and they
[7]_____ three years later in 1969. In 1970 Paul
McCartney [8]_____ the Beatles and in 1971
Lennon [9]_____ his famous solo album *Imagine*.
In 1973 Lennon [10]_____ to the USA. At 11.00
p.m. on December 8th 1980 Mark Chapman, a
Beatles fan, [11]_____ John Lennon outside his
flat in New York. He [12]_____ forty-one. [ ] 12

4 Write past simple questions.

Where *was* John Lennon *born*? In Liverpool.
1 When _____? In 1940.
2 What _____ at college? Art.
3 When _____?
   He met her in 1966.
4 Where _____ in 1973?
   To the USA.
5 How old _____ when he died? 41.
   [ ] 5

5 Write the correct tense.

I (be) in London. *I'm in London.*

> Dear Anneka,
>
> It [1](rain). I [2](sit) in a cafe in Hyde Park and I [3](write)
> you this card. We [4](stay) in a hotel near the centre.
> The hotel [5](be) very big. There [6](be) three hundred
> rooms! Every day we [7](have) breakfast in the hotel
> and then we [8](get) the bus or Underground to the
> centre. England is nice but we [9](not like) the food!
> Yesterday we [10](go) to Buckingham Palace but we
> [11](not see) the Royal family. Tomorrow morning I
> [12](buy) some presents in Oxford Street and in the
> evening we [13](see) *Cats* at the theatre.
>
> See you soon!
> Love, Alain

[ ] 13

Total [ ] 40   ✓

Fluency

1 In English, can you …?   Yes ✓

say four birthdays that you always remember. [ ]

tell a partner about what you did from 12.00 to
6.00 p.m. yesterday. [ ]

say what somebody in the room is wearing. [ ]

tell a partner your plans for tomorrow. [ ]

ask six questions about a partner's holiday. [ ]

2 What do you say?

Ask for directions to the [ ] .

Phone and ask a friend to the [ ] .

Listen to the teacher

1 Write six sentences from the story.
2 Answer the teacher's questions.

Comparatively trivial

Is Queen Elizabeth II richer than Paul McCartney?

1 Do the quiz in pairs.

Trivia quiz

History

Geography

Science

People

General knowledge

History

1 The Roman Empire was smaller than the Greek Empire.
True / False

2 World War II was shorter than World War I.
True / False

3 The Parthenon is older than the Pyramids.
True / False

4 Which technology is newer?
the silicon chip / the laser

Geography

5 Norway is bigger than Sweden.
True / False

6 The River Nile is longer than the River Amazon.
True / False

7 Which is nearer?
New York to Los Angeles / Lisbon to Istanbul

8 Which is deeper?
the Atlantic Ocean / the Pacific Ocean

Science

9 Which is heavier?
a pound (lb) / a kilogram (kg)

10 Which is hotter?
the Earth / the Moon

11 Bread is good for you, but which is better?
brown bread / white bread

12 Fat is bad for you, but which is worse?
butter / margarine

People

13 Who is richer?
Queen Elizabeth II / Paul McCartney

14 Who was younger when they died?
Marilyn Monroe / Mozart

15 Who was taller?
Stan Laurel / Oliver Hardy

16 Who was poorer when they died?
Van Gogh / Leonardo da Vinci

General knowledge

17 Which is more common in English?
'e' / 'i'

18 Which is more expensive?
Paris / Tokyo

19 Which is less valuable?
a dollar / a pound

20 Which is more dangerous?
travelling by bus / travelling by boat

Your score ▢ ▢

9

A

GRAMMAR FOCUS

Comparative adjectives + *than*

1 small	small**er**
2 big	big**ger**
3 heavy	heav**ier**
4 valuable	more / less valuable
5 bad	worse

A kilometre is shorter than a mile.
Oil is more valuable than petrol.

PRACTICE

a Find comparatives in the quiz for these adjectives.

short   good   expensive   hot   near   old   rich
common   young   dangerous

b Are they group 1, 2, 3, 4, or 5?

2 Use ▰ **Adjectives** *p.140*. Write five sentences about these actors.
Arnie's younger than Danny.

PRONUNCIATION

a ⟨ 1 ⟩ Listen. How many of your sentences do you hear?

b Listen and repeat.
/ə/ /ə/
1 *Arnie's taller than Danny.*

3 **a** What do you think?

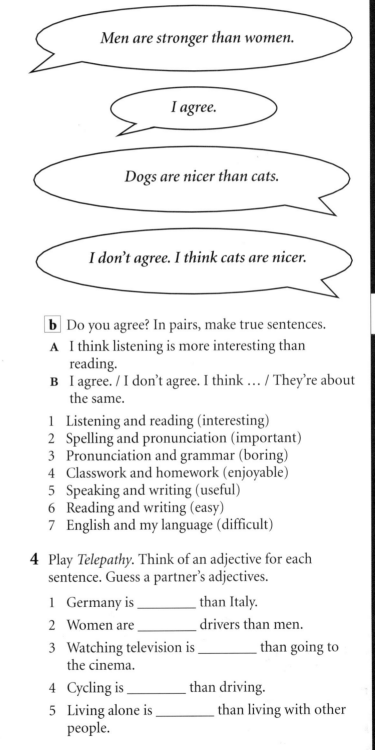

> *Men are stronger than women.*

> *I agree.*

> *Dogs are nicer than cats.*

> *I don't agree. I think cats are nicer.*

b Do you agree? In pairs, make true sentences.
A I think listening is more interesting than reading.
B I agree. / I don't agree. I think … / They're about the same.

1 Listening and reading (interesting)
2 Spelling and pronunciation (important)
3 Pronunciation and grammar (boring)
4 Classwork and homework (enjoyable)
5 Speaking and writing (useful)
6 Reading and writing (easy)
7 English and my language (difficult)

4 Play *Telepathy*. Think of an adjective for each sentence. Guess a partner's adjectives.

1 Germany is _____ than Italy.
2 Women are _____ drivers than men.
3 Watching television is _____ than going to the cinema.
4 Cycling is _____ than driving.
5 Living alone is _____ than living with other people.

Predict your future

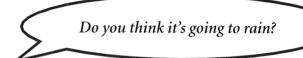

Do you think it's going to rain?

| have an accident | D | win a lot of money | ☐ | be famous | ☐ | meet a stranger | ☐ | move | ☐ |
| have a lot of children | ☐ | fall in love | ☐ | travel | ☐ | have a problem | ☐ | get a surprise | ☐ |

9

B

1 **a** Match the phrases and cards A to J.

b What do the cards mean?

A *You're going to meet a stranger.*

2 **a** ◦2◦ Boris Wood, a London taxi-driver, is with Dame Rosa. Listen. Which six cards does he choose?

1 *Card H*

b Make six sentences about Boris's future.

1 *He's going to win a lot of money.*

GRAMMAR FOCUS

Predictions: (*be*) *going to* …

● Complete the sentences.

Look at those clouds. It's going to .

You're going to fall in  .

PRACTICE

Make sentences.

3 Play *Your future.* **A** Look at the cards. Secretly number each card from 1 to 10. **B** Choose six numbers. **A** Predict **B**'s future.

4 Ask a partner about the future.
A Are you going to …?

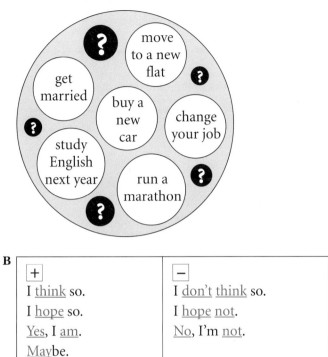

B

+	−
I think so.	I don't think so.
I hope so.	I hope not.
Yes, I am.	No, I'm not.
Maybe.	

5 **a** ◦3◦ ♫ Listen to *Three little birds*. Number the lines 1 to 7.

b He thinks today's going to be a good day. How does he know?

Happy birthday!

He's planning carefully.

1 ◦ **4** ◦ Read. Answer the questions after each paragraph.

1 7.30 a.m.

2nd June. A beautiful, sunny day. It's Clinton Grant's birthday. He's forty today. He's sitting in the bath, planning carefully. He's thinking about his new life. It's going to begin this evening, at 8.30 p.m. His plan is perfect. Clinton's thinking, 'Tonight, all that money's going to be mine!'

1 Where's Clinton Grant?
2 What's he doing?
3 What's he going to do?

2 11.00 a.m.

Clinton's in his office. He's a lawyer. His partner Barny is sitting opposite him. Clinton's thinking about Barny's money. He's smiling.
'Don't forget it's my birthday, Barny. We're going to eat at Maxine's, at 6.30. Don't be late!'
'Don't worry. I know,' answers Barny.
He's smiling happily, too. '8.30,' he's thinking.

4 What are Clinton and Barny going to do tonight?
5 Why's Barny smiling?

3 3.30 p.m.

Clinton was born forty years ago on 2nd June at 8.30 in the evening. He's very superstitious and he believes in astrology. He wants his new life to begin at 8.30 tonight. He can't be late!
Now he's standing outside a travel agency. He's looking around nervously. He doesn't want anybody to see him.
Barny's also busy. He's going shopping. He's carrying a large bag. He's smiling, too.

6 What's special about 8.30?
7 What's Clinton going to do at the travel agency?
8 What's Barny going to buy?

4 7.50 p.m.

It's a warm evening. The two partners are having dinner in the restaurant. The food's good. Barny's eating slowly. Clinton's nervous. He's looking at his watch. He's eating quickly. Forty minutes more! Is there going to be enough time? Barny asks the waiter for some matches. 'Come on, Barny,' Clinton's thinking angrily.

9   How are they feeling?
10 What's going to happen after dinner?

5 8.15 p.m.

Clinton and Barny are walking to Barny's house for coffee after dinner. The plan's working well. But it's getting late! Barny's walking slowly, too slowly. It's 8.27! Now they're standing in the garden outside Barny's house. Barny lives alone. The house is dark. Clinton's thinking fast. He's taking something out of his jacket. Barny isn't looking at him. He's looking for his keys. It's 8.30 …!

11 What's Clinton got in his jacket?
12 What's going to happen?

2 [a] ° 5 ° Listen to the end of the story. What happens?

[b] What's Clinton going to do now?

GRAMMAR FOCUS

Adverbs

● Complete the chart with these words.

carefully   nervous   slowly   nervously

Adjective	Adverb
He's a careful man. Clinton's _____. Barny's slow.	He's planning _____. He's looking around _____. He's walking _____.

● Write two letters.

We usually add _ _ to an adjective to make an adverb.

● (Circle) the adverbs in the story. Complete the chart.

1	quick carefully	quickly _____
2	happy angry	happily _____
3	good fast	well _____

PRACTICE

[a] Write the adverbs.

quiet   easy   beautiful   slow   sexy

[b] (Circle) the right word.

1   Does he drive careful / (carefully)?
2   Could you speak more slow / slowly, please?
3   My English isn't very good / well.
4   She speaks English very good / well.
5   They play chess very bad / badly.

PRONUNCIATION

[a] ° 6 ° Listen. Write five sentences.

[b] Listen again. Repeat the sentences.

3 Write six true sentences. Use adverbs.

eat   get up   speak English   drive
play tennis   cook

I eat quickly.

4 ° 7 ° Play *What's my adverb?* Listen. Write six adverbs.

9

C

Can men cook?

Do you need any meat?

The mysterious Mr Zact

Hector Zact is an accountant.
He's strange but logical.
He likes potatoes but he doesn't like pasta.
He likes onions but he doesn't like rice.
He likes biscuits but he doesn't like bread.
He likes cups and bottles but he doesn't
like tea, coffee, or water.
He likes sweets but he doesn't like sugar.

Why?

1 **a** Read the puzzle.

b Can you do the puzzle? Ask the teacher questions about Mr Zact.
Does he like fruit?

GRAMMAR FOCUS 1

Countable / uncountable nouns

● There are two kinds of noun in English.

Countable (C)	Uncountable (U)
oranges	rice
_____	_____
_____	_____
_____	_____
_____	_____

PRACTICE

a Write the nouns from the pictures in the right column.

b Look at the second column (U). Can these words be plural in your language?

2 🔊 **Food and drink** *p.135* Ask a partner.
Countable or uncountable?

3 Match the phrases on the shopping list and pictures A to J.

Shopping list			
a kilo of potatoes	G	200 grams of butter	☐
a small box of mushrooms	☐	half a kilo of tomatoes	☐
a carton of milk	☐	an onion	☐
500 grams of cheese	☐	two tins of beans	☐
a bottle of red wine	☐	three carrots	☐

Ⓒ

Ⓑ

Ⓐ

HEINZ BAKED BEANS with tomato sauce

Butter

Ⓔ

Fresh Milk

Ⓖ

Ⓕ

9

D

PRONUNCIATION

`◦ 8 ◦` Listen and repeat the shopping list. Draw the links.

1 *a kilo of potatoes*

Uncountable		Countable
milk	BUT	a carton of milk
butter		200 grams of butter

4 **a** `◦ 9 ◦` Listen to *Can men cook?* Look at the shopping list. Tick ✓ what you need to make Vegetarian Shepherd's Pie.

D

b Listen again. Write *a*, *an*, *some*, or *any*.

1 You need *a* kilo of potatoes.
2 You need _____ onion.
3 You need _____ milk.
4 You need _____ mushrooms.
5 Do you need _____ tomatoes?
6 You don't need _____ beans.
7 You don't need _____ cheese.
8 Do you need _____ meat?

H

I

J

GRAMMAR FOCUS 2

a / an / some / any

● Look at exercise 4b. Complete the chart with *some* or *any*.

		C	U
+		Use **a / an** with singular nouns. Use _____ with plural nouns.	Use _____.
− **?**		Use **a / an** with singular nouns. Use _____ with plural nouns.	Use _____.

PRACTICE

What do you need to make spaghetti bolognese? Write six sentences.

bananas   ~~onions~~   pasta   potatoes
sugar   tomatoes

1 *You need some onions.*
2 *You don't need ...*

5 **a** `◦ 10 ◦` Listen to Peter and Dorothy. Complete the form.

Home shopping form	
2 tins	beans
200 grams	_____
_____	oranges
1 kilo	_____
____ cartons	milk
1 bottle	_____
_____	bananas
1 carton	_____

Here to help you.

b Listen again. Complete Peter's questions.

1 How *many* tins of beans?
2 How _____ butter?
3 How _____ oranges would you like?
4 How _____ potatoes do you need?
5 How _____ milk do you want?
6 How _____ oil, Mrs Smith?
7 How _____ bananas?
8 How _____ orange juice, Mrs Smith?

c Role-play the phone call in pairs.

It's / They're too (big).   Buy clothes

Buying clothes

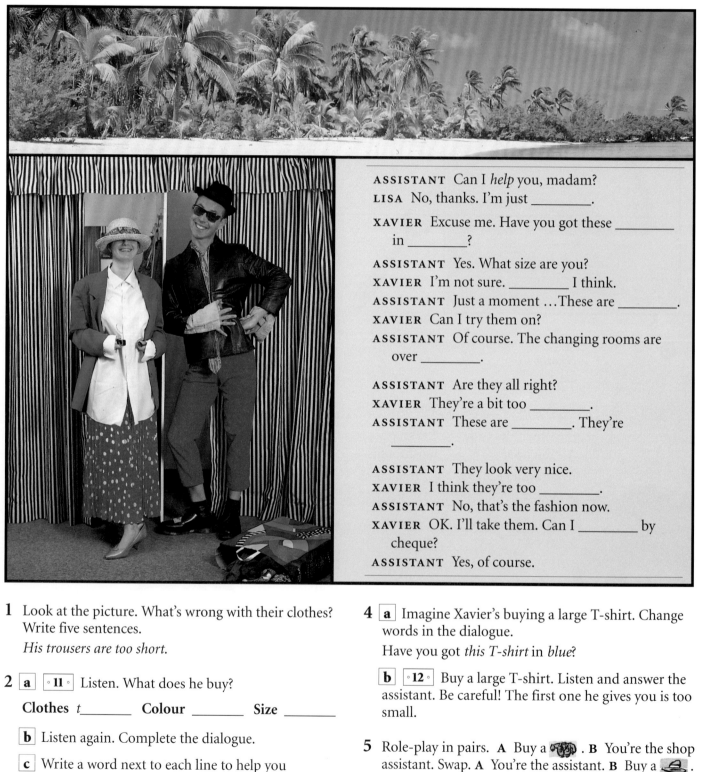

ASSISTANT Can I *help* you, madam?

LISA No, thanks. I'm just _____.

XAVIER Excuse me. Have you got these _____ in _____?

ASSISTANT Yes. What size are you?

XAVIER I'm not sure. _____ I think.

ASSISTANT Just a moment …These are _____.

XAVIER Can I try them on?

ASSISTANT Of course. The changing rooms are over _____.

ASSISTANT Are they all right?

XAVIER They're a bit too _____.

ASSISTANT These are _____. They're _____.

ASSISTANT They look very nice.

XAVIER I think they're too _____.

ASSISTANT No, that's the fashion now.

XAVIER OK. I'll take them. Can I _____ by cheque?

ASSISTANT Yes, of course.

1 Look at the picture. What's wrong with their clothes? Write five sentences.

His trousers are too short.

2 **a** ° **11** ° Listen. What does he buy?

Clothes *t*_____ **Colour** _____ **Size** _____

b Listen again. Complete the dialogue.

c Write a word next to each line to help you remember it. Practise in pairs.

3 Role-play in pairs. **A** Buy 🥿 . **B** You're the assistant. Swap. **A** You're the assistant. **B** Buy 👖 .

4 **a** Imagine Xavier's buying a large T-shirt. Change words in the dialogue.

Have you got *this T-shirt* in *blue*?

b ° **12** ° Buy a large T-shirt. Listen and answer the assistant. Be careful! The first one he gives you is too small.

5 Role-play in pairs. **A** Buy a 🐯 . **B** You're the shop assistant. Swap. **A** You're the assistant. **B** Buy a 👒 .

6 🧳 Travel phrasebook 9 *p.131*

TRAVEL WITH ENGLISH

Vocabulary file 9

1 Verbs Complete with *to, of, for, at,* or *–*.

1 Look *at* this photo.
2 I like listening _____ music.
3 Please call _____ your sister tonight.
4 Can I speak _____ Donna, please?
5 What do you think _____ Pavarotti?
6 I'm going to write _____ him tomorrow.
7 She usually goes _____ home by bus.
8 I hate waiting _____ the train.

2 Grammar words Add words for two minutes.

1 Irregular past *saw* …
2 Regular past *carried* …
3 Adverbs *slowly* …
4 Comparatives *hotter* …
5 Countable nouns *biscuit* …
6 Uncountable nouns *water* …

3 Word groups What are they?

1 station cinema town hall *They're all places.*
2 skirt jacket T-shirt
3 coffee milk orange juice
4 from opposite about
5 London LA Tokyo
6 thirsty cheap young
7 bread potatoes apples
8 pilot nurse politician

4 Prepositions Complete with by from than to .

1 It's 4,000 kms _____ LA _____ New York.
2 Sweden is bigger _____ Norway.
3 Can I pay _____ cheque?

5 English sounds Put the words in the right group.

address lawyer city does help doesn't job
light fourth revision think garage

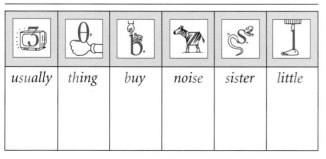

![tv]	![thumb]	![b]	![zebra]	![snake]	![lamp]
usually	*thing*	*buy*	*noise*	*sister*	*little*

Study tip

■ **Learn to read phonetics.**

Phonetics help you practise pronunciation outside class.

> **Wednesday** /ˈwenzdeɪ/ n. mercredi

Try it!

■ Match the words and phonetics.

1 Monday   /ɪkspensɪv/ ☐
2 January   /tiːtʃə/   ☐
3 teacher   /sɪnəmə/   ☐
4 expensive   /sʌmtaɪmz/   ☐
5 sometimes   /mʌndeɪ/   1
6 cinema   /dʒænjʊəri/   ☐

■ ✎ **Revision.** Choose a page from the **Word bank** *p.132.* Look only at the phonetics. Can you say and spell the words correctly?

■ Look back at all the Study tips (**Vocabulary files 1 to 9**). Which are your top three?

Grammar file 9

1 Comparative adjectives + *than*

	Adjective	Comparative	Spelling
1	old cheap	older cheaper	1 syllable + er
2	big hot	bigger hotter	1 vowel + 1 consonant → double consonant
3	happy easy	happier easier	consonant + y → ier
4	famous expensive	more famous less expensive	2 or more syllables → more / less + adjective
5	good bad	better worse	irregular

I'm taller than my brother.
My English is better than my Spanish.

☐ Use comparative adjectives + *than* to compare things.

2 Predictions: (*be*) going to …

☐ Use (*be*) + *going to* + infinitive for predictions
(= we can see what's going to happen in the future).
☐ Form of (*be*) *going to* … ▶ **Future plans** *p.100*

3 Adverbs of manner

Adjective	Adverb	Spelling
bad careful	badly carefully	+ ly
easy angry	easily angrily	consonant + y → ily
good fast	well fast	irregular

He eats quickly.
I speak French well.

☐ Adverbs describe verbs.
☐ Adverbs usually go after the verb / verb + noun
NOT ~~I speak well French.~~

4 Countable / uncountable nouns

☐ There are two kinds of noun in English:
countable (C) and uncountable (U).
☐ C = things you can count, U = things you can't count.
NOT ~~a rice~~ / ~~two butters~~

a / an / some / any

+	I'd like	an a	onion. (C) tomato. (C)
−	I don't want		
?	Do you need		
+	I'd like We need	some	coffee. (U) potatoes. (C)
−	We don't need We haven't got	any	butter. bananas.
?	Have you got	any	rice? oranges?

☐ Use *a / an* + C singular nouns.
☐ Use *some* + C plural nouns and U nouns in [+].
☐ Use *any* + C plural nouns and U nouns in [?] and [−].
☐ Remember: use *some* in questions to offer or ask
for things.
Would you like **some** coffee?
Can I have **some** water, please?

How much …? / How many …?

How much	coffee money	do you want?
How many	potatoes cups of coffee	

☐ Use *How much …?* + U nouns.
☐ Use *How many …?* + C plural nouns.

a lot of

I eat a lot of bananas.
She drinks a lot of coffee.

☐ Use *a lot of* with C and U nouns.

112

▶ Workbook *p.57* Do **Grammar check** 9.

Love at first sight

1 Read and guess the percentages. Compare with a partner.

12%   5%   2%   18%   40%   23%

> *City Life* magazine interviewed 1,000 couples. These were the results.
>
> 💜 **Where did you meet your partner for the first time?**
>
> ☐ _____ met their partner at school / university.
>
> ☐ _____ met through friends.
>
> ☐ _____ met at a party or disco.
>
> ☐ _____ met in the street / on a bus / train, etc.
>
> ☐ _____ met at work.
>
> ☐ _____ said they couldn't remember!
>
> 💜 **Do you believe in love at first sight?**
>
> 58% said they did.

2 a ○ 1 ○ Listen to *Love at first sight*. Do you know any shows like this?

b ○ 2 ○ Listen. What did Carla ask Emma?

3 a Listen again. Write Emma's answers.

Emma	Gary
1 *to the cinema*	☐
2 _____	☐
3 _____	☐
4 _____	☐
5 _____	☐

b ○ 3 ○ Listen. Are Gary's answers the same? Tick ✓ or cross ✗.

4 In groups, write more questions to ask on *Love at first sight*.

Was it love at first sight? What did you eat on your first date? Did you kiss goodbye?

5 Play *Love at first sight* with the teacher.

6 a Read the song. Guess the picture words.

Song

1 The first time ever I saw your 🖼️

2 I thought the ☀️ rose in your 👁️

3 And the 🌙 and the ⭐ were the 🎁 you gave

4 To the _____ and endless ✨, my ❤️

5 And the first 🕐 ever I 💃 your 👄

6 I felt the 🌍 move in my ✋

7 Like the trembling 💚 of a captive 🕊️

8 That was there at my command

b ○ 4 ○ 🎵 Listen and check. How did she feel when she first met him?

Famous for five decades

THE ENGLISH FILE QUESTIONNAIRE

Biography

Cliff Richard (real name Harry Webb) was born in India on 14th October 1940, and came to Britain at the age of eight. In July 1959, he had his first number one with the Shadows, *Living Doll*. Of his 113 singles, 62 were Top Ten hits. He had Top Ten hits in the 50s, 60s, 70s, and 80s, and he's still making hit records now. He's single and has no children. Each year, he gives a lot of money to charity. He's richer than the Queen.

Profile

First name	*Cliff*
Surname	_____
Date of birth	_____
Nationality	*British*
Place of birth	_____
Marital status	_____
Children	_____

Possessions

Q Have you got a car?
A Yes, I've got three: a Rolls Royce, a Mercedes 500 SL, and a Range Rover.

Q Have you got any pets?
A Two dogs, Amy and Misty.

Q Which is your favourite room in your house?
A The library / TV room.

Lifestyle

Q Do you smoke?
A No, I don't.

Q What do you have for breakfast?
A Toast, and tea or coffee.

Q What do you always carry with you?
A Usually keys and a credit card, and not much else!

Q What was your first job?
A I worked in an office.

Q Are you a good manager of time?
A No! I leave that to other people.

Q What do you like doing in your spare time?
A Playing tennis.

Q What foreign languages do you speak?
A None.

Q Can you play a musical instrument?
A The guitar.

Tastes

Q Where did you go for your last holiday?
A I went skiing in Austria.

Q What are you reading at the moment?
A *Wuthering Heights*, by Emily Brontë.

Q What sports do you do?
A I play tennis and I ski.

Q What's your favourite drink?
A Chardonnay wine.

Q What's your favourite food?
A Indian.

Q Who are your favourite actors?
A Robert de Niro and Meryl Streep.

Q Who are your favourite musicians?
A James Burton and John Clark (guitarists).

Q What's your favourite record?
A *Heartbreak Hotel*, by Elvis Presley.

Plans

Q Where are you going to go for your next holiday?
A Portugal.

Q What are you going to do when you retire?
A Nothing – but I'll be busy doing it!

Interview by Angela O'Leary

1 Look at the photos. What do you know about him?

2 **a** Read the biography. Complete the profile.

b What were the questions?
What's your first name?

3 Read the interview. Do any answers surprise you?

4 **a** Imagine the teacher's answers to the questions.

b Interview the teacher to check.

5 Interview a partner. Write the answers.

° 5 ° ♫ *Summer holiday*, Cliff Richard

Around the world

1 📖 Play *Phrasebook* in groups. **A** Choose a phrase from the **Travel phrasebook** *p.130*. Describe when you need to use it. **B**, **C**, and **D** Guess the exact phrase. Swap.

  A You're in a restaurant. You want to pay. What do you say to the waiter?

  D 'Could I have the bill, please?'

2 6 Listen to the dialogues. Match them to three pictures.

3 Play *Line of four* in teams. Ask the teacher.

Jealous!

> *Have you ever been to Thailand?*
> *No, I haven't.*

1 **a** ° 7 ° Listen. Who's David? Does Oliver like him?

b Listen again. Complete the chart.

	1	2	3
1 Which countries has Ann been to?	*Italy*		
2 When did she go there?			
3 Who did she go with?			

GRAMMAR FOCUS 1

Present perfect

● Use *have* + past participle.

+			−		
I you we they	've	been	I (etc.) haven't		been
he she it	's		he (etc.) hasn't		

?			✓ ✗	
Have I (etc.)	been ?		Yes, I have. No, I (etc.) haven't.	
Has he (etc.)			Yes, he has. No, he (etc.) hasn't.	

Have you ever been to Bangkok? I've been to Bangkok twice.	= present perfect
When did you go to Bangkok? I went to Bangkok ten years ago.	= past simple

● Write 'past simple' or 'present perfect'.

We use the _____ when the time isn't important.

We use the _____ when we say / ask 'when'.

Ann and Oliver are trying to decide where to go on holiday.

OLIVER Have you ever been to 🏳️?

ANN Yes, I have. I went there ⚽.

OLIVER Really? Who did you go with?

ANN With David.

OLIVER Oh, David. Of course. Well, have you been to 🏳️?

ANN Only for a weekend.

OLIVER When was that?

ANN Oh, I don't know. 📅, I think.

OLIVER Don't tell me. With David?

PRACTICE

Make present perfect sentences.

1 I / been / Greece.
   I've been to Greece.
2 He / never been / Turkey.
3 / you ever been / Japan? Yes, I /.
4 / they ever been / Egypt? No, they /.
5 We / been / France three times.

10
C

The Parthenon

Tower Bridge

The Colosseum

The Eiffel Tower

The Statue of Liberty

The Great Wall of China

PRONUNCIATION

○ 8 ○ Listen to sentences 1 to 5. Repeat.

1 *I've been* (/bɪn/) *to Greece.*

2 Ask about a) the places in the pictures and b) local places. Find five places a partner has visited.

A Have you (ever) been to New York?
B Yes, I have. / No, I haven't.
A When did you go there?

GRAMMAR FOCUS 2

Past participles

● Regular verbs have the same form as the past simple.

Infinitive	Past simple	Past participle
work	worked	worked
play	played	played
study	studied	studied
I've worked in Italy. Have you ever studied Greek?		

● Irregular verbs have irregular past participles.

Infinitive	Past simple	Past participle
be	was / were	been
drive	drove	driven
make	made	made
Have you been to Rio? I haven't made a pizza before.		

PRACTICE

Circle the past participle. Write the infinitive. Regular or irregular?

1 She's written a new song. *write – irregular*
2 We've never tried Japanese food.
3 He hasn't taken many photos.
4 Have they found a new flat?
5 I've forgotten my homework.

3 **a** Complete the questions with the participles.

met ~~seen~~ written read won lived

Have you ever …

1 *seen Casablanca?*
2 _____ a famous person?
3 _____ in another country?
4 _____ *War and Peace?*
5 _____ a competition?
6 _____ a song or a poem?

b Interview a partner. Ask more questions, too.

A Have you ever seen *Casablanca?*
B Yes, I have.
A Where …? When …? Who / with?

4 **a** Write five *Have you ever…?* questions.

b Interview a different partner.

10

C

117

Communication

Student A

1 C · Famous names?

a Ask **B** questions about pictures 2, 4, 6, and 8.
Complete the chart.
What's his / her real name? How do you spell it?
Where's he / she from?

Famous names	Elton John	Sting
First name	Reginald	
Surname	Dwight	
From	Britain	

Tina Turner	Whoopee Goldberg	Michael Caine
Annie		Maurice
Bullock		Micklewhite
the USA		Britain

George Michael	Cher	Bob Dylan
	Cherilyn	
	Sarkisian	
	the USA	

b Listen to **B**. Answer the questions about pictures 1, 3, 5, and 7.
His / Her first name / surname is …   He's / She's from …

1 D · Phone numbers

a Ask **B** questions. Complete the information.
What's number 2? What's the phone number?

	Important phone numbers		
○			
○		① The hospital	☎ 540631
○		② _____	☎ _____
○		③ The dentist	☎ 349880
○		④ _____	☎ _____
○		⑤ The bus station	☎ 857134
○		⑥ _____	☎ _____
○		⑦ The post office	☎ 477008
○		⑧ _____	☎ _____

b Listen to **B**. Answer the questions.
It's the hospital. It's five four oh six three one.

1 E · Questions and answers

a Test **B**. Ask questions 1 to 8.
Are Fiat and Armani Italian?

1 / *Fiat* and *Armani* Italian? (✔)
2 / *Elizabeth Taylor* American? (✘ British)
3 / *IBM* and *Kodak* British? (✘ American)
4 / *Alain Delon* and *Gerard Depardieu* French? (✔)
5 / *Luciano Pavarotti* Spanish? (✘ Italian)
6 / *Chanel* and *Dior* Egyptian? (✘ French)
7 / *Steven Spielberg* German? (✘ American)
8 / *Sony* and *Honda* Japanese? (✔)

b Listen to **B**. Answer the questions.
Yes, he / she is. OR No, he / she isn't. He's / She's …
Yes, they are. OR No, they aren't. They're …

2 A · How many …?

a Ask **B** questions. Complete the information.
How many cameras?

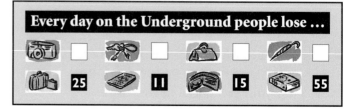

Every day on the Underground people lose …

25   11   15   55

b Listen to **B**. Answer the questions.

3 ◁▷   Day trip

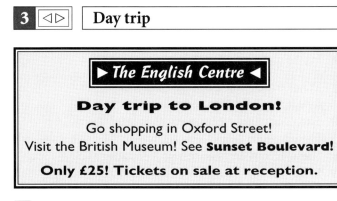

▶ The English Centre ◀

Day trip to London!

Go shopping in Oxford Street!
Visit the British Museum! See **Sunset Boulevard!**

Only £25! Tickets on sale at reception.

a   Ask **B** questions. Complete the information.
What time does …? / What time do …?

The bus …

leaves the school	....	.... a.m.
arrives in London	....	10.45 a.m.
leaves London	....	11.00 p.m.
gets back to the school	....	.... a.m.

The British Museum
- opens .... a.m.
- closes 5.00 p.m.

The Tower of London
- opens 9.30 a.m.
- closes .... p.m.

The National Gallery
- opens .... a.m.
- closes 6.00 p.m.

banks
- open .... a.m.
- close 3.30 p.m.

shops
- open 9.00 a.m.
- close .... p.m.

Sunset Boulevard
- starts 8.00 p.m.
- finishes .... p.m.

b   Listen to **B**. Answer the questions.

5 C   *How often do you …?*

a   Interview **B**. Complete the chart.

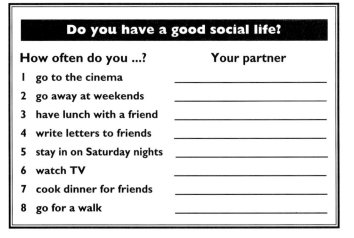

Do you have a good social life?

How often do you …?	Your partner
1 go to the cinema	....
2 go away at weekends	....
3 have lunch with a friend	....
4 write letters to friends	....
5 stay in on Saturday nights	....
6 watch TV	....
7 cook dinner for friends	....
8 go for a walk	....

b   Answer **B**'s questions.

6 A   *What do you think of …?*

a   Write three 'interesting' names in each group.
Harrison Ford / boxing / Japanese, etc.

Famous people
1 _____ ☐
2 _____ ☐
3 _____ ☐

Sports
1 _____ ☐
2 _____ ☐
3 _____ ☐

International food
1 _____ ☐
2 _____ ☐
3 _____ ☐

TV programmes
1 _____ ☐
2 _____ ☐
3 _____ ☐

Local places
1 _____ ☐
2 _____ ☐
3 _____ ☐

b   Interview your partner.
What do you think of Harrison Ford ?
Note the answers. Use these symbols.

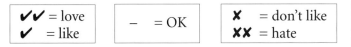

| ✔✔ = love | | ✘   = don't like |
| ✔   = like | –   = OK | ✘✘ = hate |

6 B Find ten differences

Ask about **B**'s picture. Find ten differences.
Is / Are there ...?   Where is it / are they?   How many ...?

◄ **on the left**   **in the middle**   **on the right** ►

6 D Murder!

a Complete your questions about James Harvey's study with *was* or *were*.

1 What colour _____ the carpet? (red)
2 How many pictures _____ there on the wall? (one)
3 _____ there two plants in the room? (no, one)
4 _____ the glass on the floor? (no, on the desk)
5 How many cigarettes _____ there in the ashtray? (two)
6 Where _____ the pens? (in a cup, on the desk)
7 _____ there a knife on the floor? (no, in James Harvey)

b Test **B** and **C**. Give a point for each right answer.

c Answer **B** and **C**'s questions.

6 ◁▷ Sell your house

You want to sell your house / flat.

a Read the advert. Think about the information you want to give.

> *Better* ▦ *Homes*
>
> Do you want to sell your house?
> We give a very good price and a quick sale.
> **Phone us today on (01865) 69700.**

b Phone **B** at Better Homes.
Hello. I'd like to sell my ...
Answer **B**'s questions.

8 🔍 Question practice

a Write questions 1 to 10.

1 What time / wake up? (3.00 a.m.)
   What time did they wake up?
2 Next morning / get up early or late? (early)
3 How / get to work? (by train)
4 (be) / happy in / morning? (no, angry)
5 What (be) in / car? (red roses and an envelope)
6 Why / man take / car? (because his mother was ill)
7 / go to Manchester by train? (no, by car)
8 Where / go after dinner? (to the theatre)
9 / get home from Manchester / 12.30 a.m? (no, 1.00 a.m.)
10 How / feel when / got home? (tired and happy)

b Ask pair **B** questions 1 to 10.

c Answer pair **B**'s questions.

8 ◁▷ The end of the story?

a Read and remember your story in two minutes.

Story 1
Terri left the bar. Then she caught a train to Canada. When she arrived in Montreal she met Chris. Chris was Terri's sister. She was a doctor. They went to Chris's house. They talked for a long time. Then Chris phoned John. John got the first plane to Montreal. John said, 'I love you. Please come back with me to London.' Terri said, 'I need more time.' Two months later Terri went back to John in London.

b Tell your story to **B** and **C**.

c Listen to **B** and **C**.

d Which do you like best, story 1, 2, or 3? Tell **B** and **C**.

Student B

1 C Famous names?

a Listen to **A**. Answer the questions about pictures 2, 4, 6, and 8.

His / Her first name / surname is …
He's / She's from …

b Ask **A** questions about pictures 1, 3, 5, and 7. Complete the chart.

What's his / her real name? How do you spell it?
Where's he / she from?

1 D Phone numbers

a Listen to **A**. Answer the questions.
It's the doctor. It's double three one oh eight three.

	Important phone numbers		
①	_____	📞	_____
②	The doctor	📞	331083
③	_____	📞	_____
④	The airport	📞	949634
⑤	_____	📞	_____
⑥	The station	📞	780225
⑦	_____	📞	_____
⑧	The police station	📞	632659

b Ask **A** questions. Complete the information.
What's number 1? What's the phone number?

1 E Questions and answers

a Listen to **A**. Answer the questions.
Yes, he / she is. OR *No, he / she isn't. He's / She's …*
Yes, they are. OR *No, they aren't. They're …*

b Test **A**. Ask questions 9 to 16.
Are CNN and MTV American?

9 / CNN and MTV American? (✔)
10 / Julio Iglesias Brazilian? (✘ Spanish)
11 / spaghetti and pizza French? (✘ Italian)
12 / Robert de Niro Italian? (✘ American)
13 / Mercedes and BMW Polish? (✘ German)
14 / Jodie Foster and Whitney Houston American? (✔)
15 / Yoko Ono Chinese? (✘ Japanese)
16 / Camembert and Brie Spanish? (✘ French)

2 A How many …?

a Listen to **A**. Answer the questions.

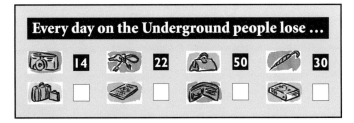

b Ask **A** questions. Complete the information.
How many cases?

3 ◁▷ Day trip

a Listen to **A**. Answer the questions.

The bus ...

leaves the school	8.30 a.m.
arrives in London .... _____	a.m.
leaves London .... _____	p.m.
gets back to the school	1.00 a.m.

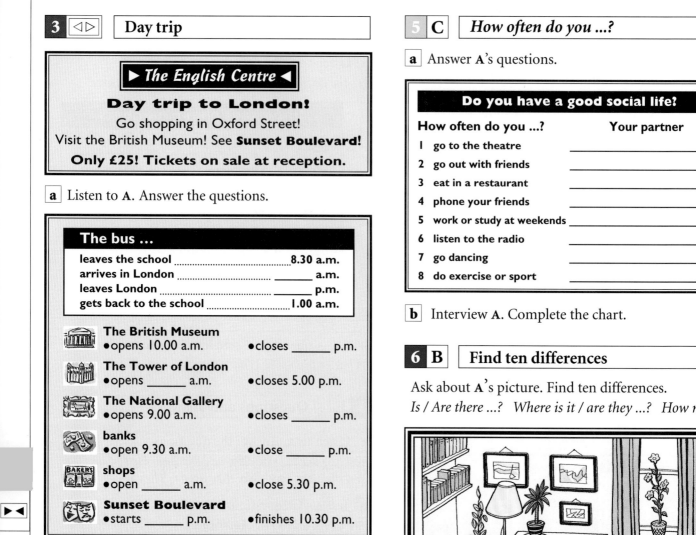

The British Museum
- opens 10.00 a.m.
- closes _____ p.m.

The Tower of London
- opens _____ a.m.
- closes 5.00 p.m.

The National Gallery
- opens 9.00 a.m.
- closes _____ p.m.

banks
- open 9.30 a.m.
- close _____ p.m.

shops
- open _____ a.m.
- close 5.30 p.m.

Sunset Boulevard
- starts _____ p.m.
- finishes 10.30 p.m.

b Ask **A** questions. Complete the information.
What time does ...? / What time do ...?

5 C *How often do you ...?*

a Answer **A**'s questions.

Do you have a good social life?

How often do you ...?	Your partner
1 go to the theatre	_____
2 go out with friends	_____
3 eat in a restaurant	_____
4 phone your friends	_____
5 work or study at weekends	_____
6 listen to the radio	_____
7 go dancing	_____
8 do exercise or sport	_____

b Interview **A**. Complete the chart.

6 B Find ten differences

Ask about **A**'s picture. Find ten differences.
Is / Are there ...? Where is it / are they ...? How many?

◀ on the left ═ in the middle ═ on the right ▶

6 D Murder!

a Complete your questions about James Harvey's study with *was* or *were*.

1 ____ there a cushion on the chair? (no)
2 ____ there an envelope on the desk? (yes)
3 ____ there any books on the desk? (yes, an address book)
4 How many keys ____ there in the picture? (three)
5 How many pieces of paper ____ there on the floor? (two)
6 What ____ the time? (7.15)
7 Where ____ the plant? (on the second shelf)

b Answer **A**'s questions.

c Test **A** and **C**. Give a point for each right answer.

d Answer **C**'s questions.

6 ◁▷ Sell your house

You're an estate agent. You work for Better Homes.

a What questions do you need to ask to complete the form?
How many (rooms) are there? Has it got (central heating)? Is it (near the centre)?

```
┌─────────────────────────────────────────────┐
│              Better ⊞ Homes                  │
│  ┌────────────────────────────────────────┐ │
│  │ Surname ............  First name ......  │ │
│  │ Address ...............................  │ │
│  │ Telephone .............................  │ │
│  └────────────────────────────────────────┘ │
│  ┌────────────────────────────────────────┐ │
│  │ Details:                                 │ │
│  │ house  ☐                                 │ │
│  │ flat   ☐   which floor  ☐               │ │
│  │ age    ☐   years old                    │ │
│  │                                          │ │
│  │ number of rooms ☐  bedrooms ☐  bathrooms ☐│ │
│  │                                          │ │
│  │ central heating ☐   a garage ☐   a lift ☐│ │
│  │ a garden ☐          a phone ☐           │ │
│  │                                          │ │
│  │ near the centre ☐   quiet ☐    modern ☐ │ │
│  │                                          │ │
│  │ other information .......................│ │
│  └────────────────────────────────────────┘ │
└─────────────────────────────────────────────┘
```

b Answer the phone. Interview **A**. Complete the form.

8 🔍 Question practice

a Write questions 11 to 20.

11 / Eric or Brenda call / police? (Brenda)
   Did Eric or Brenda call the police?
12 / walk to / station? (no, they ran)
13 / get home at 5.00? (no, at 6.00)
14 Where / find / car in / evening? (outside the house again)
15 What (be) in / envelope? (a letter and two tickets)
16 What (be) / name at the end of / letter? (Tony)
17 Where / have dinner? (in a French restaurant)
18 What show / see in Manchester? (*The Phantom of the Opera*)
19 Where / park / car that night? (outside the house)
20 What / find in / house? (nothing)

b Answer pair **A**'s questions.

c Ask pair **A** questions 11 to 20.

8 ◁▷ The end of the story?

a Read and remember your story in two minutes.

Story 2

Terri left the bar. Then she caught a train to Canada. When she arrived in Montreal she met Chris. Chris was a girl in Terri's class at school. They were good friends. Chris was the editor of a newspaper. Terri said, 'I want to start a new life in Montreal.' Chris said, 'I have a job for you.' Terri never went back to London. She never saw her husband again.

b Listen to **A**.

c Tell your story to **A** and **C**.

d Listen to **C**.

e Which do you like best, story 1, 2, or 3? Tell **A** and **C**.

Student C

6 D Murder!

a Complete your questions about James Harvey's study with *was* or *were*.

1 _____ there a watch on the desk? (yes)
2 _____ there a packet of cigarettes on the desk? (no)
3 How many pens _____ there in the picture? (three)
4 _____ the windows open or closed? (open)
5 What _____ the picture in the room? (a woman)
6 What colour _____ the curtains? (green)
7 Where _____ the keys? (on the envelope, in the door)

b Answer **A** and **B**'s questions.

c Test **A** and **B**. Give a point for each right answer.

8 ◁▷ The end of the story?

a Read and remember your story in two minutes.

Story 3

Terri left the bar. Then she caught a train to Canada. When she arrived in Montreal she met Chris. Chris was Terri's first boyfriend. They met in Prague ten years ago. He was an American journalist. They kissed. He said, 'Ten years is a long time.' She said, 'I love you.' Terri never saw her husband again.

b Listen to **A** and **B**.

c Tell your story to **A** and **B**.

d Which do you like best, story 1, 2, or 3? Tell **A** and **B**.

Listening

1 B · 11 ·

1 RECEPTIONIST Good afternoon, sir.
DIETER Good afternoon. My name's Dieter Uhlmann. I have a reservation.
RECEPTIONIST How do you spell Uhlmann?
DIETER U-H-L-M-A-double N.
RECEPTIONIST Your room number's 342.
DIETER Thank you very much.

2 MONA Good morning.
RECEPTIONIST Good morning, madam. Can I help you?
MONA Yes, I have a reservation.
RECEPTIONIST What's your name, please?
MONA Badawi. Mona Badawi.
RECEPTIONIST How do you spell your surname?
MONA B-A-D-A-W-I.
RECEPTIONIST Sorry. Can you repeat that, please?
MONA Yes. B-A-D-A-W-I.
RECEPTIONIST And your first name?
MONA Mona. M-O-N-A.
RECEPTIONIST Right. Thank you. You're in room 207, Ms Badawi.

1 E · 23 ·

MIKE Good morning. What's your name, please?
RUSSELL Russell Di Napoli.
MIKE Where are you from?
RUSSELL The USA.
MIKE So you speak English.
RUSSELL Yes, of course.
MIKE Seat number C7.
RUSSELL Thanks.

ANA Hello. My name's Ana Martin.
MIKE What nationality are you, please?
ANA I'm Spanish.
MIKE Do you speak English, Ms Martin?
ANA Yes, no problem.
MIKE Your seat number is D14.
ANA OK, thank you.

MIKE Good morning. Where are you from?
MRS OTAWA We're from Japan.
MIKE And your names, please?
MRS OTAWA Mr and Mrs Otawa.
MIKE Do you speak English?
MRS OTAWA No, not very well.
MIKE Don't worry. Channel 9's in Japanese. Your seats are E3 and E4.

1 · 28 ·

BEN Good afternoon.
LI Good afternoon.
TANYA Hello.
BEN Seat numbers 17E and 18E. Thank you.
LI Thank you.
TANYA Thanks.

CAPTAIN Welcome aboard British Airways flight BA 654. Please fasten your seat belts and …

BEN Anything to drink, madam?
TANYA Yes, coke, please.
BEN With ice and lemon?
TANYA Yes, please.
BEN Here you are. And for you, sir?
LI Tea, please.
BEN Milk and sugar?
LI No, thanks.
BEN Lemon?
LI Oh. Yes, please.
BEN Here you are.
LI Thank you very much.

LI Goodbye.
BEN Goodbye.
TANYA Thanks. Bye.
BEN Goodbye, madam.

OFFICIAL Passports, please. Thank you. Welcome to Mexico City.

2 D · 17 ·

WOMAN Do you work or study?
MAN I work.
WOMAN What do you do?
MAN I'm an engineer.
WOMAN Where do you work?
MAN In Kuwait.
WOMAN Do you like your job?
MAN It's OK. The money's good.

MAN Do you work or study?
WOMAN I study.
MAN What do you study?
WOMAN French, German, and English.
MAN Where do you study?
WOMAN Milan University.
MAN Do you like your course?
WOMAN Yes, I do, very much.

2 · 21 ·

1 SAMI Good morning. Can I change $140 into pounds, please?
CASHIER $140. Yes. That's £70.
SAMI Sorry?
CASHIER £70.
SAMI Thank you.

2 ARZU Excuse me. How much is this dictionary?
SHOP ASSISTANT £19.
ARZU £90?
SHOP ASSISTANT No, nineteen.
ARZU Oh, that's OK.

3 TAXI DRIVER Where to?
SAMI How much is it to the city centre?
TAXI DRIVER £40.
SAMI 14?
TAXI DRIVER No, forty. Four oh. Forty.
SAMI Oh, OK.

4 ARZU Two cokes, please!
BARPERSON Here you are.
ARZU How much is that?
BARPERSON £5.80.
ARZU Pardon?
BARPERSON Five pounds eighty.
ARZU OK, OK. Here you are.

3 D · 15 ·

1 MADELEINE Oh, no! It's half past seven! I'm late!

2 RADIO DJ This is Steve Wright on the Breakfast Special and the time now on Radio 1 is seventeen minutes to eight.
MADELEINE Oh, I'm really late.

3 ANNOUNCER The next train is the 8.22 fast service to Paddington. I repeat … the next train is the 8.22 fast service to Paddington.

4 MADELEINE Taxi! …
Do you have the right time, please?
TAXI DRIVER Yes, love. It's a quarter past nine.

MADELEINE A quarter past nine? Oh no. Please hurry! I'm late!
TAXI DRIVER Right.

5 MAN Madeleine! It's five to ten! Come on!

6 MADELEINE Good morning. It's ten o'clock and this is Madeleine Black with the news on ATV.

3 · 17 ·

RECEPTIONIST Good morning. Western Hotel. How can I help you?
HARRY Can I make a reservation, please?
RECEPTIONIST Yes, sir. When for?
HARRY Next Tuesday. The fourth.
RECEPTIONIST Yes, of course. What name, please?
HARRY Wells. Harry Wells.
RECEPTIONIST How do you spell that?
HARRY W-E-double L-S.
RECEPTIONIST W-E-L-L-S. OK, Mr Wells. Would you like a single room or a double?
HARRY How much is a double room?
RECEPTIONIST It's $150 a night, including breakfast.
HARRY And a single room?
RECEPTIONIST $120 a night, including breakfast.
HARRY Do all the rooms have a shower?
RECEPTIONIST Yes, sir. They have a shower and a bath. This is a four star hotel.
HARRY Can I have a single room, please?
RECEPTIONIST Yes, of course. How many nights would you like to stay?
HARRY Three, please.
RECEPTIONIST What's your address, Mr Wells?
HARRY 110 Oxford Street, 2041 Sydney, Australia.
RECEPTIONIST And your phone number?
HARRY Sydney 02 8185452.
RECEPTIONIST Sydney 02 8185452. And your nationality? Are you Australian?
HARRY No, I'm not. I'm Canadian.
RECEPTIONIST OK. That's fine, Mr Wells. A single room for three nights from next Tuesday.
HARRY Yes, that's right. Thank you.
RECEPTIONIST You're welcome, Mr Wells. See you on Tuesday. Goodbye.
HARRY Goodbye.

3 · 20 ·

Edinburgh Festival information for 9th August.

The Military Tattoo at Edinburgh Castle is at 7.45 and 10.45 p.m. Tickets from £7.50 to £15.

Theatre: *Death in Venice* at the Hill Street Theatre is at 1.30 p.m. Tickets £5.00.

Cinema: *I'm not a feminist but …* at the Film House is at 2 p.m. Tickets £3.

Music: Chinese music at the Queen's Hall is at 6.30 p.m. Tickets £4.50.

4 C · 8 ·

SUE Hello. Mr Harding? My name's Sue Wright. I'm here about my insurance …
MR HARDING Yes. Good afternoon. Come in. Please sit down. Just one or two questions. What do you do?
SUE I'm a teacher.
MR HARDING Are you married?
SUE Yes, I am.

124

MR HARDING OK. Have you got a TV?
SUE Yes, I have.
MR HARDING Have you got a video?
SUE No, I haven't.
MR HARDING Have you got a stereo?
SUE Yes, I have. I've got a Sony.
MR HARDING And a computer?
SUE Yes, I've got a Macintosh.
MR HARDING Have you got a video camera?
SUE No, I haven't.
MR HARDING Have you got a fax?
SUE Yes, I have.
MR HARDING Have you got a car?
SUE Yes, it's a Renault.
MR HARDING And a bike?
SUE No, I haven't.
MR HARDING Good. Now let's see … oh, it's quite cheap …

4 C · 12 ·

Twenty years later and Stan Bowles is unemployed. 'I haven't got anything now. I haven't got a job. I haven't got a house or a car. I live in my friend's flat. I'm divorced. I smoke eighty cigarettes a day. And I haven't got any money in the bank. I still gamble. I'm poor but I'm happy!'

Twenty years later and Anita Roddick is rich. She's now a multi-millionaire and she's got two houses. Her company, The Body Shop, is world famous and she's got 1,213 shops in forty-five countries. Anita says, 'I've got a wonderful job. I'm very happy.'

4 D · 16 ·

INTERVIEWER Good evening, and welcome to *In your free time*. Tonight's guest is the actress Elaine Dixon. Hello, Elaine.
ELAINE Hello.
INTERVIEWER Have you got a lot of free time, Elaine?
ELAINE Oh no, not enough!
INTERVIEWER What do you like doing?
ELAINE Oh, a lot of things.
INTERVIEWER For example?
ELAINE I love painting.
INTERVIEWER Painting? That's interesting.
ELAINE And I like reading very much. I really like reading in the bath.
INTERVIEWER In the bath?
ELAINE Yes! It's very relaxing!
INTERVIEWER What kind of books do you read?
ELAINE Well, I really like romantic novels.
INTERVIEWER What about music?
ELAINE I love listening to all kinds of music. Rock, classical music, jazz – everything.
INTERVIEWER Do you like watching TV?
ELAINE No, I don't. I hate watching TV.
INTERVIEWER Why?
ELAINE Because it's really boring!
INTERVIEWER What about sports?
ELAINE I don't do any sports, but I like swimming when I've got the time.
INTERVIEWER Do you like cooking?
ELAINE Cooking? Oh, I hate it!
INTERVIEWER Why?
ELAINE Because I'm a terrible cook. Ask my children.

4 ⌂ · 19 ·

1 RIAZ Hello. How much are those envelopes?
   ASSISTANT Ten piastres each.
   RIAZ Can I have ten, please? And have you got any camera batteries?

ASSISTANT Yes. Could I see your camera? OK. Here you are.
RIAZ How much are they?
ASSISTANT Two pounds each. Do you need a film?
RIAZ No, thanks. Just the batteries. How much is that?
ASSISTANT That's five pounds. Thank you. Have a good holiday.
RIAZ Thanks a lot. Bye.

2 ANA How much is that box?
   OWNER This one?
   ANA No, that small one.
   OWNER This one. It's very cheap. One thousand pounds.
   ANA Thanks. Goodbye.
   OWNER Wait a moment. A special price for you – eight hundred pounds.
   ANA No, thanks.
   OWNER How much?
   ANA It's OK. I don't want it, thanks.
   OWNER Five hundred pounds. Last price.
   ANA No, thanks. Bye.
   OWNER OK. How much?
   ANA Two hundred pounds.
   OWNER What! Oh, no, no …
   ANA Thanks a lot. Goodbye.
   OWNER Wait! OK. Four hundred pounds.
   ANA Three hundred.
   OWNER Three hundred and fifty.
   ANA OK. Three hundred and fifty. Here you are.

3 ASSISTANT Yes?
   RIAZ Could I have a packet of aspirins, please?
   ASSISTANT Here you are. Anything else?
   RIAZ Have you got any toothbrushes?
   ASSISTANT Yes, these are five pounds and those are seven pounds fifty.
   RIAZ One of those, please. How much is that?
   ASSISTANT Five pounds eighty for the aspirins and seven pounds fifty for the toothbrush. That's thirteen pounds thirty, please.
   RIAZ Here you are. Thanks a lot.

4 ◁▷ · 21 ·

ALAN How old's your sister, Danny?
DANNY Jane? She's twenty-seven.
ALAN Is she married?
DANNY Yeah, she is. We're all married now!
ALAN Has she got any children?
DANNY Yeah, she's got a little boy, Billy. He's horrible! Jane's very good-looking. She's got very long blond hair and brown eyes. She's very tall, too.
ALAN Mm. What does she do?
DANNY She's a dancer.
ALAN What, ballet?
DANNY No, modern dance. She's in Moscow now. She travels a lot.
ALAN Does she like her job?
DANNY Yeah. She loves dancing and she really likes travelling, so she's very happy.
ALAN But she's married.
DANNY Yeah, sorry.

4 ◁▷ · 22 ·

How about you?
I like New York in June
How about you?
I like a Gershwin tune
How about you?
I love a fireside
When a storm is due
I like potato chips

Moonlight and motor trips
How about you?
I'm mad about good books
Can't get my fill
And James Durante's looks
Give me a thrill
Holding hands in the movie show
When all the lights are low
May not be new
But I like it
How about you?

5 A · 1 ·

Suzy Stressed gets up late and has a shower. She doesn't have breakfast. She goes to work by car. She gets to work at five to nine. She uses the lift. At eleven o'clock she has a cigarette and a black coffee. Suzy has lunch at half past one. She finishes work at six o'clock. Then she goes to an Italian class. She gets home late. After that she watches TV. She has dinner at eleven o'clock. She goes to bed very late. Suzy is very stressed. Do you live like Suzy?

5 A · 3 ·

This is Henry Healthy's day. Henry gets up early. He goes running before breakfast. Then he has a shower. He has fruit juice and cereal for breakfast. After that he walks to work. He doesn't use the lift. He starts work at half past nine. He goes home at five o'clock. In the evening he does yoga. Henry doesn't watch TV. He goes to bed early. Henry is very healthy. Do you live like Suzy or Henry?

5 C · 7 ·

INTERVIEWER How often do you go to the cinema, Teresa?
TERESA It depends. I usually go three or four times a month.
INTERVIEWER And how often do you go to a disco?
TERESA About four or five times a month. I love dancing!
INTERVIEWER What kind of music do you like?
TERESA Salsa.
INTERVIEWER Do you go to dance classes?
TERESA Yes, I do. Once or twice a week. When I've got enough money!
INTERVIEWER How often do you go to church?
TERESA I go every Sunday.
INTERVIEWER Do you often go away at weekends?
TERESA It depends. In the summer I go away a lot. My parents have got a flat near the beach. So I usually go away about nine or ten times a year.
INTERVIEWER And how often do you go for a walk?
TERESA Nearly every day. Usually with my boyfriend after work. Then we have a drink or see a film.

5 ⌂ · 11 ·

WAITER Good afternoon.
MAN A table for three, please.
WAITER Come this way.

WAITER Are you ready to order now?
WOMAN Yes. Could I have garlic mushrooms?
MAN Garlic mushrooms for me too, please.
GIRL I don't like garlic. I want soup.
WAITER And for your main course?
WOMAN Could I have seafood pasta, please?
MAN Steak for me, please.
GIRL I don't like salad, or pasta, or steak. I want chips.

WAITER Yes, of course. So that's one seafood pasta, one steak and chips, and one … chips. What would you like to drink? Beer, wine, mineral water?
MAN Wine, I think. Red, white, or rosé?
WOMAN Red for me.
MAN OK. Can we have two glasses of red wine?
GIRL And I want coke.
WAITER Yes, of course … Is that OK?
MAN Yes, fine.

GIRL Mum, my soup's cold.
WOMAN Excuse me. This soup is cold.
WAITER Oh, I'm terribly sorry.

WAITER Is everything OK now?
MAN Yes, fine. Have you got a light?
WAITER Yes. Here you are. Would you like anything else?
GIRL Chocolate mousse, chocolate mousse, I want chocolate mousse.
WOMAN Nothing for me, thanks.
MAN Coffee?
WOMAN Yes, please.
MAN OK. Just two coffees, a chocolate mousse, and the bill, please.

MAN Excuse me. I think the bill is wrong. Look.

5 🖻 · 12 ·

MAN Excuse me. I think the bill is wrong. Look. We had two coffees, not three.
WAITER Oh?
GIRL Yeah, I had chocolate mousse, not coffee.
WAITER Oh! I'm very sorry.
MAN No problem.

5 ◁▷ · 13 ·

Anything you want
Every time I look into your loving eyes
I see love that money just can't buy
One look from you I drift away
I pray that you are here to stay

Anything you want, you've got it
Anything you need, you've got it
Anything at all, you've got it
Baby

Every time I hold you I begin to understand
Everything about you tells me I'm your man
I live my life to be with you
No one can do the things you do

Anything you want, you've got it
Anything you need, you've got it
Anything at all, you've got it
Baby

I'm glad to give my love to you
I know you feel the way I do

Anything you want, you've got it
Anything you need, you've got it
Anything at all, you've got it
Baby

6 A · 1 ·

PRESENTER Hi! Welcome to *Is it a hit?* On *Is it a hit?* we play this week's new records. Then the audience tell us what they think. A hit or a miss. And the first record is *A funny feeling* by The Nerd. … OK, so let's ask our audience. What do you think of *A funny feeling*, madam?
WOMAN 1 It's terrible! I don't like it. It's really boring. One point.
PRESENTER And you, sir?
MAN 1 I like it. I think it's very good. Three points.
PRESENTER And you, madam?

WOMAN 2 It's all right. I quite like it. It's interesting but nothing special. Two points.
PRESENTER And you?
MAN 2 I love it. I think it's great! Brilliant! Five points!
PRESENTER Madam?
WOMAN 3 I'm sorry. It's awful! I hate it. No points!
PRESENTER So, that's only eleven points. I'm sorry, The Nerd, but this audience thinks *A funny feeling* is a miss.

6 B · 6 ·

Your song
It's a little bit funny
This feeling inside
I'm not one of those who can easily hide
Don't have much money but, boy, if I did
I'd buy a big house where we both could live

If I was a sculptor, but then again, no …
Or a man who makes potions in a travelling show
I know it's not much but it's the best I can do
My gift is my song and this one's for you

And you can tell everybody this is your song
It may be quite simple but now that it's done
I hope you don't mind, I hope you don't mind
That I put down in the words how wonderful
    life is
While you're in the world

So excuse me forgetting but these things I do
You see, I've forgotten if they're green or they're
    blue
Anyway, the thing is, what I really mean
Yours are the sweetest eyes I've ever seen
And you can tell everybody …

6 C · 8 ·

NARRATOR This week's True Crime Story is 'Murder at Christmas'. It's Christmas Day, 1948, in a large house near Oxford. It's James Harvey's house. James Harvey is an international businessman. It's a cold evening. The house is full of family and friends.
ALISON James, it's Alison. Dinner's ready … James, everybody's here … James? Are you there, James? … James? Aaaaaaaagh! Help!

6 D · 13 ·

NARRATOR The Inspector interviews Simon Harvey.
INSPECTOR Well, Simon. Where were you yesterday evening at 7.00?
SIMON I was in the living-room.
INSPECTOR Who were you with?
SIMON I was with my mother.
INSPECTOR Did you like your father?
SIMON What?
INSPECTOR Did you like your father?
SIMON Of course I did.
INSPECTOR Are you sure?
SIMON Of course I'm sure! Listen, Inspector. I didn't murder my father. I loved him. He was a wonderful man.
INSPECTOR Thank you, Simon. No more questions.

NARRATOR The Inspector interviews Ingrid Harvey.

INSPECTOR So, Miss Harvey. Where were you at 7.00 on Christmas Day?
INGRID I was in the garden.
INSPECTOR Who were you with?
INGRID I was with Geoffrey.
INSPECTOR Geoffrey?

INGRID Yes, Geoffrey Smith.
INSPECTOR Are you and … Geoffrey good friends?
INGRID He's a friend of the family. Everybody likes Geoffrey.
INSPECTOR Thank you, Miss Harvey.
NARRATOR The Inspector interviews Geoffrey Smith.
INSPECTOR Come in, Mr Smith. Whisky?
GEOFFREY Yes, thanks.
INSPECTOR Here you are. Now, Mr Smith. Where were you at 7.00 yesterday?
GEOFFREY Yesterday? I was – I was in the garden with Ingrid.
INSPECTOR Were you and Mr Harvey friends, Mr Smith?
GEOFFREY Yes, yes, we were. We were very good friends.
INSPECTOR Very good friends, Mr Smith?
GEOFFREY Yes, Inspector. For twenty years.
INSPECTOR Hm. Thank you, Mr Harvey.

6 🖻 · 16 ·

ARCHIE It's a bit expensive. What about the bus?
JANA Just a moment. There's a bus at 6.30 in the morning. It arrives at 3.00 in the afternoon.
SITA That's eight and a half hours!
ARCHIE How much is it?
JANA It's 750 crowns single and 1,500 crowns return.
SITA Is there a toilet on the bus?
JANA Yes, and there's a video, food, drinks …
SITA What about the plane?
JANA The first plane is at 9.20 in the morning. It arrives at 10.40. But it's 6,000 crowns single and 12,000 crowns return.
ARCHIE Hm. That's a lot. What do you think, Sita?

6 🖻 · 17 ·

ARCHIE Hm. That's a lot. What do you think, Sita?
SITA The plane's really quick.
ARCHIE Yeah. But it's very expensive. What about the bus? It's got a video and a toilet –
SITA But it's eight and a half hours! I hate travelling by bus.
ARCHIE All right. Let's get the train.
SITA OK.
ARCHIE Thank you very much for your help.
JANA You're welcome. Have a nice time in Budapest.

6 🖻 · 18 ·

1 SITA Two tickets, please.
   ASSISTANT That's 400 forints, please. Would you like a guidebook?
   SITA How much are they?
   ASSISTANT 800 forints.
   ARCHIE No, thanks.

2 ARCHIE Oh. I'm sorry.
   MAN That's OK.
   ARCHIE Are you all right?
   MAN Yes, don't worry. I'm fine.
   ARCHIE I am sorry.
   MAN It's OK. Really.

3 ARCHIE Two return tickets to Budapest, please.
   ASSISTANT That's 6,000 crowns, please.
   ARCHIE Can I pay by credit card?
   ASSISTANT Yes, sir. Thank you.
   ARCHIE Which platform?
   ASSISTANT Platform 4.

4 ARCHIE Phew! It's hot. Can you pass the water, please? Thanks.
SITA More cheese?
ARCHIE No, thanks. I'm fine.
SITA The Danube is really beautiful.
ARCHIE Yes. What a wonderful holiday! Cheers!
SITA Cheers!

6 ◁▷ ° 19 °

ESTATE AGENT Good afternoon, Better Homes. Can I help you?
MRS JONES Good afternoon. I'm phoning about your advert in the paper.
ESTATE AGENT Er, which one?
MRS JONES The house near Oxford, reference 4782. How much is it?
ESTATE AGENT Just a moment. Let me see. It's … £140,000.
MRS JONES How big is it?
ESTATE AGENT Oh, it's very big.
MRS JONES How many rooms has it got?
ESTATE AGENT It's got four bedrooms, a very large kitchen, a study, a living-room, a dining-room, and three bathrooms. So that's … eleven rooms.
MRS JONES Has it got a garden?
ESTATE AGENT Yes, it's got a very big garden. And a large garage, for three cars.
MRS JONES Where is it exactly?
ESTATE AGENT It's in the country, about thirteen kilometres from Oxford.
MRS JONES Thirty?
ESTATE AGENT Er, no. Thirteen.
MRS JONES Good. I work in Oxford. Is there a swimming pool?
ESTATE AGENT Yes, there is. And there's central heating in the house.
MRS JONES Is there any furniture?
ESTATE AGENT No, there isn't. The house is empty.
MRS JONES Is there a phone?
ESTATE AGENT Er, no.
MRS JONES Has it got a tennis court?
ESTATE AGENT Er, no, it hasn't. But it's got a sauna.
MRS JONES I see. How old is it?
ESTATE AGENT It's about ninety years old. Would you like to see it?
MRS JONES Yes, please.
ESTATE AGENT Is Friday afternoon OK?
MRS JONES Yes. What time?
ESTATE AGENT At 5.45. Outside our office in Oxford.
MRS JONES That's fine. 5.45 on Friday. Thank you. Goodbye.

6 ◁▷ ° 20 °

ESTATE AGENT Here we are. Now this is the hall.
MR JONES It's very big!
MRS JONES It's a very big house, darling.
ESTATE AGENT Follow me … In here we have the kitchen.
MR JONES It's a bit old.
MRS JONES It's an old house, darling.
ESTATE AGENT The house is ninety years old, sir … And this is the living-room.
MR JONES Oh, this is nice.
MRS JONES Yes, very nice …
ESTATE AGENT And this is one of the bathrooms.
MR JONES Ugh, it's a bit dirty.
ESTATE AGENT Follow me … The Harvey family lived here for sixty years. This was Mr Harvey's study.

MRS JONES It's very cold in here.
MR JONES Yes, very cold.
ESTATE AGENT The house has got central heating, madam.
MRS JONES Brrr. I – I don't like this house.
ESTATE AGENT Why not, madam?
MRS JONES I don't know. Ugh! There's something I don't like – there's something horrible … No, I'm sorry! Come on. Let's go.
ESTATE AGENT But madam –
MR JONES But darling –
MRS JONES Sorry, but I don't like the house. Thank you.

7 A ° 2 °

CLARE Well, Mr Marlow. Did you follow Sarah last Friday?
MARLOW Yes, I did.
CLARE Where did she go, Mr Marlow?
MARLOW Hey, call me Dick.
CLARE Just answer my questions, Marlow.
MARLOW OK, Ms Devane, relax. She went out at about 8.00 a.m. She didn't go to work. First she went swimming. Then she had breakfast in a café. After that she –
CLARE But did she have a cigarette?
MARLOW No, she didn't.
CLARE Are you sure?
MARLOW Yes, I am.
CLARE All right. What did she do after that?
MARLOW Well, first she went to the bank. Then she went shopping. At 11.15 a.m. she went to the hairdresser's. She was in there for two hours! After that she went to a restaurant. She had lunch with a tall, dark man.
CLARE Charlie! He smokes! Did she have a cigarette?
MARLOW No, I'm sorry, Ms Devane, she didn't.
CLARE What did she do then?
MARLOW At 4.00 p.m. she went to the gym for an hour. Then she went to a café and had a drink …

7 B ° 8 °

MONA Hello. Mona Badawi.
SOPHIE Hi, Mona. It's me, Sophie. Happy birthday to you, happy birthday –
MONA Thanks, but my birthday was on Saturday!
SOPHIE Yes, I know. Sorry! Did you have a good time?
MONA Yes, it was great!
SOPHIE Where did you go?
MONA We went out. We went to a Greek restaurant.
SOPHIE Who did you go with?
MONA With Ahmed and some friends.
SOPHIE What did you have to eat?
MONA Moussaka, and then a wonderful chocolate cake.
SOPHIE What did you do after that?
MONA We had a party. We danced and sang. It was lovely.
SOPHIE Oh, good.
MONA But what about your weekend, Sophie? What did you do?
SOPHIE Oh, nothing special.
MONA No?
SOPHIE No, I didn't go out this weekend. I stayed in.
MONA Oh, Sophie. Why did you stay in? …

7 C ° 9 °

1 JIM Morning, Mr North. Cold today, isn't it?
MIKE Good morning, Jim. Could I have the *Financial Times*, please?

JIM Here you are.
MIKE Thanks.

2 MIKE Good morning, Sheila.
SHEILA Good morning, Mike.
MIKE Are there any messages for me?
SHEILA Yes, there's a fax from France.
MIKE Thanks. Mm. From Sophie Villeneuve. Anything else?
SHEILA There's a letter from the bank.
MIKE Oh dear.

3 ASSISTANT Who's next?
MIKE A Big Mac please.
ASSISTANT Yes, sir. Fries?
MIKE No, thanks.
ASSISTANT Anything to drink?
MIKE A large orange juice, please.

4 MIKE Good afternoon. How much are those roses?
MAN £20.
MIKE What, each?
MAN No, sir! They're £20 for twelve.
MIKE OK. I'd like twelve, please.
MAN Certainly, sir. What colour would you like?
MIKE Red, I think. Can I pay by cheque?
MAN Yes, of course.

5 MIKE A single to the airport, please.
MAN £2.40.
MIKE Here you are. Thanks.

6 WOMAN Good afternoon, sir.
MIKE Good afternoon.
WOMAN Your ticket and passport, please. Thank you. Have you got any hand luggage?
MIKE No, I haven't.
WOMAN Go to gate number 33. Boarding in fifteen minutes. Have a good flight.
MIKE Thank you.

7 C ° 14 °

1 ANNOUNCER Good morning. It's 8.00 on Friday 28th June. The news, read by Richard Cross.

2 ANSWERPHONE Sorry, I'm not here at the moment. Please leave a message after the beep.
JULIA Hello, Martyn. This is Julia. It's Saturday, Saturday the 9th. The 9th of March. Could you ring me when you get in, please? Please Martyn. Please ring me.

3 MAN Right, here are your tickets. Two returns to Glasgow for 3rd August. The train leaves at 7.30 in the morning and arrives at 9.15. Have a good trip.

4 WOMAN Good evening. How much are tickets to see the London Symphony Orchestra?
MAN £22.50. But we've only got tickets for 12th July. Is that OK?
WOMAN The 12th? Yes, that's fine. Could I have four, please?
MAN Yes, of course. Can I have your credit card number?

5 WOMAN Good afternoon. Can I help you?
MAN Yes, I want to change these traveller's cheques.
WOMAN Certainly, sir.
MAN OK. Er, what's the date today?
WOMAN It's 30th October.
MAN The 30th. Thank you. Here you are.

7 🛄 ° 22 °

1 TOURIST Excuse me, please. Where's the station?
MAN It's in South Street, opposite the town hall.
TOURIST Thanks.

127

2 **TOURIST** Excuse me. Is there a bank near here?
WOMAN A bank? Yes, over there, next to the museum.

3 **TOURIST** Excuse me. Do you speak English?
WOMAN Yes, of course.
TOURIST Is there a market near here?
WOMAN Yes, there is. Let's see. There's one in Central Avenue. On the corner of East Street. Opposite the lake.

4 **TOURIST** Er, excuse me.
MAN Yes?
TOURIST Do you know this town?
MAN Yes.
TOURIST Is there a cheap restaurant near here?
MAN Well, there's a McDonald's in North Road. Between the police station and the language school.
TOURIST Thank you very much.

7 ⏸ · 23 ·

TAXI DRIVER Which way now?
TOURIST Go straight on. OK. Turn right at the music shop. Good. Turn right at the traffic lights. Right! Not left!
TAXI DRIVER Sorry. Now where?
TOURIST Go past the lake. Now turn left there. OK. Stop here. This is my hotel. Here on the right! Stop! Thank you. How much is that?

7 ⏸ · 24 ·

TOURIST Could you tell me the way to the station?
MAN Yes, of course. Go straight on. Turn left. Go past the town hall and it's on the right.
TOURIST Er, could you say that again, please?
MAN Go straight on. Turn left. Go past the town hall. It's on the right.
TOURIST Sorry. I don't understand. Could you speak more slowly, please?
MAN Go straight on. Then turn left. Go past the town hall. It's on the right. OK?
TOURIST Er, could you show me on the map?
MAN Yes, look.

7 ◁▷ · 25 ·

1 **BOB** When was the last time you went to a wedding?
MICK Six, no, wait a minute, seven years ago.
BOB What wedding was that?
MICK It was my wedding!

2 **AGNES** When was the last time you cried at the cinema?
KIM A long time ago. When I saw *Love Story*. Do you remember? You were with me.
AGNES Oh yes, I cried too. That was a really sad film.

3 **GILL** When was the last time you had a holiday?
DES I can't remember.
GILL You see! You work too much.
DES No, I don't. Oh, yes. I remember now. I went to Germany for two weeks.
GILL When was that?
DES About eight years ago.

7 ◁▷ · 26 ·

MAN
WOMAN Oh, no!

MR PIKE Hello. Can I help you?
WOMAN Oh! You're English! We need to get to Boulogne.

MR PIKE Don't worry. I can take you to Paris. Then you can get the train. Come on.
MAN Thank you very much.

MR PIKE Look. There's the station. Gare du Nord. That means 'North Station'.
WOMAN Wow. Your French is very good, Simon.
MR PIKE Thank you. Now, you wait here. I can get the tickets for you.
MAN Oh, thanks. Here's some money.
WOMAN He's very friendly.
MAN Yes, very friendly.

MR PIKE Here are your tickets. Now let's see. Which platform is it? Excusez-moi?
GUARD Oui, monsieur?
MR PIKE Ou est le quai pour Boulogne?
GUARD Bologna?
MR PIKE Oui.
GUARD Cest là-bas. Numéro sept. Mais vite, vite, vite! Il part toute de suite.
MR PIKE Merci. Platform seven. Hurry up. It's leaving.
MAN Right. Come on, dear.

WOMAN Well, goodbye Simon. And thank you very, very much.
MAN Thank you, Simon. Goodbye.
MR PIKE Au revoir!
WOMAN Goodbye.

WOMAN Ah, what a nice man!
MAN Yes.
WOMAN What time do we arrive in Boulogne?
MAN I don't know. Perhaps these people know. Er, excuse me. Do you speak English?
ITALIAN Hello. Yes, I speak a little English. Football. Manchester United. Arsenal.
MAN What time does the train – this train – arrive in Boulogne?
ITALIAN In Boulogne? No, my friend. Not Boulogne. I think you have a problem. This train is going to Bologna. Bologna, in Italy.
MAN
WOMAN Oh, no!

8 B · 6 ·

… is wearing blue jeans with a brown belt, a green T-shirt, and trainers. This was the fashion in the …

… is wearing a grey jacket and skirt. She's wearing a small black hat and black shoes. Her hair is short. This was the fashion in the …

8 ⏸ · 14 ·

1 **JOE** Oh no!

2 **WOMAN** 6524467.
JOE Hello. Is that Donna?
WOMAN Who?
JOE Can I speak to Donna, please?
WOMAN Who?
JOE Donna. Donna Rice.
WOMAN I'm sorry. I think you've got the wrong number.
JOE What number's that?
WOMAN 6524467.
JOE Oh, I'm sorry.

3 **ANSWERPHONE** This is 6523467. I'm sorry I can't take your call. Please leave a message after the beep.
JOE Hello, Donna. This is Joe Hansen from San Francisco. That's H-A-N-S-E-N. I'm a friend of Bill's. I've got a message for you from Bill. I'm staying at the Carlton Hotel. The number is 7996083, room 501. Please call me tonight. Thank you. Bye.

8 ⏸ · 15 ·

RECEPTIONIST Carlton Hotel. Good evening.
DONNA Could I speak to Mr Joe Hansen in room 501, please?
RECEPTIONIST Just a moment, please.
JOE Hello?
DONNA Is that Joe Hansen?
JOE Speaking.
DONNA Hello, Joe. This is Donna Rice.
JOE Donna! Listen! I've got an important message for you from Bill.
DONNA Oh, what is it?
JOE Just a moment. Remember. It's from Bill. Listen. 'I just called to say Bill loves you. I just called to say how much he cares. I just called to say Bill loves you. And he means it from the bottom of his heart.'
DONNA Thanks, Joe. That was beautiful!

8 ⏸ · 16 ·

I just called to say I love you
No New Year's Day to celebrate
No chocolate-covered candy hearts to give away
No first of spring, no song to sing
In fact, here's just another ordinary day

No April rain, no flowers bloom
No wedding Saturday within the month of June
But what it is, is something true
Made up of these three words that I must say to you

I just called to say I love you
I just called to say how much I care
I just called to say I love you
And I mean it from the bottom of my heart

9 B · 2 ·

BORIS I'm Boris Wood.
ROSA Ah, come in, my dear. Let me take your coat.
BORIS Thank you.
ROSA Please, sit down.
BORIS Thank you.
ROSA Good. Now, you're going to choose six cards. These six cards tell us your future. All right?
BORIS Right. One, two, three, four, five, and one more, six.
ROSA Ah. Hm. Hmmm.
BORIS What can you see? Is it good?
ROSA Listen to me carefully, my dear. The first card is money. I see money. A lot of money. You're going to get a lot of money, my dear.
BORIS Oh, good. I hope so. But when? How much?
ROSA Ah. Sssh. The second card. You're going to meet someone. You're going to meet an important person, a very famous person … very soon.
BORIS Is it a man or a woman?
ROSA I see a tall, dark man.
BORIS Is it Bruce Springsteen?
ROSA I'm sorry, I don't know his name. The third card says you're going to travel. You're going to travel very far.
BORIS Of course I'm going to travel. I'm a taxi driver!
ROSA Are you married, my dear?
BORIS No, I'm not.
ROSA Well, you're going to fall in love and get married very soon.
BORIS What? No! That's impossible! I haven't got a girlfriend!
ROSA The next card says children. A lot of children. You're going to have a lot of children.
BORIS Oh no! I hate children. Are you sure?

ROSA The cards are never wrong, my dear. Now, the last card. Very soon you're going to get a surprise.

BORIS What kind of surprise? A nice surprise?

ROSA A surprise is a surprise, Mr Wood. I can't say more. Well, that's all.

BORIS Thank you. Thank you very much. That was very interesting. Er, how much is that?

ROSA That's £60, please. Cash or American Express.

BORIS £60! Impossible! It was only five minutes!

ROSA Those are my prices, my dear. I'm a professional.

BORIS £60! I don't believe it. £60 for five minutes. Huh! So is that my surprise?

9 D · 9 ·

BOB Welcome to *Can men cook?* Hello, my name's Bob, and – Can men cook?

AUDIENCE Yes, they can!

BOB Well, Amanda, who's our first guest tonight?

AMANDA This is Colin and he's from Bristol!

BOB Hello, Colin! Well, Colin, what are you going to cook tonight?

COLIN Vegetarian Shepherd's Pie.

BOB And what do you need, Colin?

COLIN You need some potatoes –

AMANDA About a kilo.

COLIN An onion.

AMANDA A big one.

COLIN Some milk and butter –

AMANDA Just a little.

COLIN Some mushrooms –

AMANDA A small box.

COLIN Some carrots –

AMANDA Three big ones.

BOB Do you need any tomatoes?

COLIN Yes, you do. But you don't need any beans or any cheese in my recipe.

BOB Do you need any meat, Colin?

COLIN No, Bob. It's vegetarian. And finally, I always have –

AMANDA A nice bottle of Italian red wine to drink with it.

BOB Thank you, Amanda. And so, the question is – Can men cook?

AUDIENCE Yes, they can!

BOB Colin, how do you make Vegetarian Shepherd's Pie?

COLIN Well, Bob, first you …

BOB OK. It's time to take the Vegetarian Shepherd's Pie out of the oven. And it looks … delicious, er … I'm going to ask Amanda to try it! Well, Amanda? What do you think of it? Can men cook?

AMANDA Mm. Well, Colin, it's – it's – it's very – nice.

9 D · 10 ·

PETER Peter Patel, customer services. Can I help you?

DOROTHY Oh, hello, Peter. This is Dorothy. Dorothy Smith.

PETER Hello, Mrs Smith. How are you today?

DOROTHY Not too bad.

PETER Good. Now, what do you need this week?

DOROTHY Well, I'd like some beans.

PETER How many tins of beans?

DOROTHY Two tins, please. And some butter.

PETER How much butter?

DOROTHY Oh. Ah. Er …

PETER 200 grams?

DOROTHY Oh, yes, 200. And some oranges, please.

PETER OK, Mrs Smith. How many oranges would you like?

DOROTHY Er, four please, Peter. And I'd like some potatoes as well.

PETER How many potatoes do you need?

DOROTHY Oh. Er …

PETER A kilo?

DOROTHY Yes, a kilo. And some milk.

PETER Some milk, Mrs Smith. How much milk do you want? Two cartons?

DOROTHY Er, yes, two cartons, please. And some, er, some oil.

PETER How much oil, Mrs Smith?

DOROTHY A bottle, please. And some bananas.

PETER How many bananas?

DOROTHY Six.

PETER Is that everything?

DOROTHY Yes. No. I want some orange juice.

PETER How much orange juice, Mrs Smith? A carton?

DOROTHY Yes, a carton, please. Well, that's everything. Thank you very much, Peter.

PETER Thank you, Mrs Smith.

10 A · 1 ·

ANNOUNCER And here's your host, Carla Black!

CARLA Hello! I'm Carla Black. Welcome to *Love at first sight*. Each week we ask a couple five questions. If their answers are exactly the same, they win a holiday. And this week's holiday for two is in … Hawaii! And our first couple tonight is Emma and Gary. First, ladies and gentlemen, let's meet Emma. …

10 A · 2 ·

CARLA First, ladies and gentlemen, let's meet Emma. … Now, Emma. Just five questions. Number one. The easy question. Where did you go on your first date? Can you remember?

EMMA Yes, we went to the cinema and we saw *Batman*!

CARLA OK. And question number two. Where did you meet Gary?

EMMA We met at a bus stop in Oxford Street.

CARLA At a bus stop in Oxford Street? Very romantic. Question number three. When exactly did you meet? Can you remember?

EMMA Yes, I can. It was 3rd February 1994.

CARLA 3rd February. OK. And the fourth question. What did you say to Gary? The first thing?

EMMA Yes, Carla, I remember. I said, 'Excuse me! What time is the next bus?'

CARLA OK. And finally, question five. What did Gary say?

EMMA Gary said, 'I don't know.'

CARLA Thank you, Emma.

10 A · 3 ·

CARLA And now it's your partner's turn. Let's welcome Gary, ladies and gentlemen! … Hello, Gary.

GARY Hi.

CARLA Now Gary, think carefully. If you answer the same as Emma, you win the holiday in Hawaii. The first question. Where did you go on your first date? Can you remember?

GARY We saw a film, I think, at the cinema. Yeah, Kim Basinger. Jack Nicholson. What was it called? *Batman*!

CARLA Correct! Where did you meet Emma for the first time?

GARY It was at a bus stop, Carla – in – in Oxford Street.

CARLA Correct! When did you meet?

GARY When? The exact date? It was 1994. February. I think it was the 4th. No, the 3rd!

CARLA Correct! OK, Gary. The fourth question. When you met at the bus stop, what did Emma say?

GARY Yeah, I remember what she said. She said, 'Excuse me! What time's the next bus?'

CARLA Correct! And now the final question, ladies and gentlemen. Gary, question number five, for the dream holiday in Hawaii. What did you say to Emma?

GARY I said, 'You've got beautiful eyes!'

CARLA I'm sorry, Gary, that's not the right answer.

EMMA Oh, Gary! You didn't say that! Oh, you're so stupid! You said, 'I don't know!' Oh, you stupid, stupid man …

10 B · 5 ·

Summer holiday

We're all going on a summer holiday
No more working for a week or two
Fun and laughter on our summer holiday
No more worries for me or you
For a week or two

We're going where the sun shines brightly
We're going where the sea is blue
We've seen it in the movies
Now let's see if it's true

Everybody has a summer holiday
Doing things they always wanted to
So we're going on a summer holiday
To make our dreams come true
For me and you

We're going where the sun shines brightly
We're going where the sea is blue
We've seen it in the movies
Now let's see if it's true

Everybody has a summer holiday
Doing things they always wanted to
So we're going on a summer holiday
To make our dreams come true
For me and you

10 · 6 ·

1 WOMAN Good afternoon. Your ticket, please. Thank you. How many bags have you got?

KEIKO These two.

WOMAN Aisle or window?

KEIKO Could I have a window seat?

WOMAN And smoking or non-smoking?

KEIKO Non-smoking.

WOMAN Let's see. OK. Seat 15F. Boarding at 5.15, please. Gate 14.

KEIKO Gate 14? Thanks a lot.

WOMAN Have a good flight.

2 OFFICIAL Can I see your passport, please?

JUAN Here you are.

OFFICIAL That's fine. Thank you.

3 FLIGHT ATTENDANT Would you like chicken or fish?

KEIKO Fish, please.

FLIGHT ATTENDANT And what would you like to drink?

KEIKO Coke, please. And could I have a glass of water?

Travel phrasebook

How do you say these phrases in your language?

1 ⊞ *On the plane*

Your language

Hello.

Yes, please.

No, thanks. / No, thank you.

Nothing for me.

Thank you very much.

You're welcome.

Sorry? / Pardon?

Goodbye.

2 ⊞ *How much is that?*

Can I change *$150*, please?

Do you have a pen?

Just a moment.

Here you are.

Can I have *a steak sandwich*, please?

Anything else?

How much is that?

Excuse me.

3 ⊞ *At the hotel*

Do you have any rooms, please?

Can I make a reservation, please?

Would you like a *single room*?

How much is a *double room*?

Where's the lift?

It's over there.

How much is it a night?

A *single* room for *three* nights.

4 ⊞ *Tourist shopping*

Do you speak English?

Could I have *ten stamps* for *Italy*?

Have you got any *envelopes*?

Do you have any *camera batteries*?

How much is this / that *box*?

How much are these / those *envelopes*?

One of these / those, please.

Thanks a lot.

5 ⊞ *At the restaurant*

A table for *two*, please.

I'd like *garlic mushrooms*, please.

Could I have *vegetable soup*?

Seafood pasta for me, please.

Have you got a light?

Could we have the bill, please? _____

Can I pay by credit card? _____

Excuse me. I think the bill is wrong. _____

6 📖 *At tourist information*

We'd like to go to *Budapest* on *Friday*. _____

We'd like to go by *train*. _____

What time does the first *plane* leave? _____

What time does it arrive? _____

Is there a toilet on the bus? _____

A single / return to *Budapest*, please. _____

Which platform? _____

I'm sorry. / Sorry. _____

That's OK. _____

Cheers. _____

7 📖 *Directions*

Excuse me please, where's the *station*? _____

Is there a *bank* near here? _____

Could you tell me the way to the *station*? _____

Go straight on, past the *church*. _____

Then turn *right* at the *traffic lights*. _____

Could you say that again, please? _____

I'm sorry. I don't understand. _____

Could you speak more slowly, please? _____

Could you show me on the map? _____

8 📖 *On the phone*

Hello. Could I speak to *Donna*, please? _____

It's engaged. _____

I'll call back later. _____

I think you've got the wrong number. _____

Please call me *tonight*. _____

Is that *Joe*? _____

Speaking. _____

This is *Donna*. _____

9 📖 *Buying clothes*

I'm just looking. _____

Have you got *these trousers* in *brown*? _____

What size are you? _____

Can I try it / them on? _____

Where are the changing rooms? _____

It's / They're a bit too *big*. _____

OK. I'll take it / them. _____

Can I pay by cheque? _____

1 Countries, nationalities, and languages

Flag	Country	Nationality	Language
One syllable			
	France	French	French
	Greece	Greek	Greek
-ish			
	Britain	British	English
	Poland	Polish	Polish
	Spain	Spanish	Spanish
	Sweden	Swedish	Swedish
	Turkey	Turkish	Turkish
-an			
	Germany	German	German
	Mexico	Mexican	Spanish
	The (United) States	American	English
-ian			
	Argentina	Argentinian	Spanish
	Australia	Australian	English
	Brazil	Brazilian	Portuguese
	Egypt	Egyptian	Arabic
	Italy	Italian	Italian
	Hungary	Hungarian	Hungarian
	Nigeria	Nigerian	English
	Russia	Russian	Russian
-ese			
	China	Chinese	Chinese
	Japan	Japanese	Japanese
	Portugal	Portuguese	Portuguese
	_____	_____	_____
	_____	_____	_____

1 Use CAPITAL letters for countries, languages, and nationalities.
2 Great Britain = England, Scotland, and Wales.
3 The United Kingdom (The UK) = England, Scotland, Wales, and Northern Ireland.

2 Numbers

A

1 one /wʌn/
2 two /tuː/
3 three /θriː/
4 four /fɔː/
5 five
6 six
7 seven
8 eight /eɪt/
9 nine
10 ten
11 eleven
12 twelve
13 thirteen /θɜːtiːn/
14 fourteen
15 fifteen
16 sixteen
17 seventeen
18 eighteen
19 nineteen
20 twenty
21 twenty-one
22 twenty-two

B Write the numbers.

30	thirty
	thirty-three
	forty-four
	fifty-five
	sixty-six
	seventy-seven
	eighty-eight
	ninety-nine
	a hundred /ə hʌndrəd/
	a hundred and one
	a hundred and twenty-five
	two hundred
	nine hundred and ninety-nine
	a thousand /ə θaʊznd/
	a million /ə mɪlɪən/

3 Places

A Match the places and pictures 1 to 13.

1	airport /eəpɔːt/
	bus /bʌs/ station
	car park
	cinema
	disco
	hospital
	hotel
	market
	police station
	post office /pəʊst ɒfɪs/
	restaurant /restrɒnt/
	school /skuːl/
	station

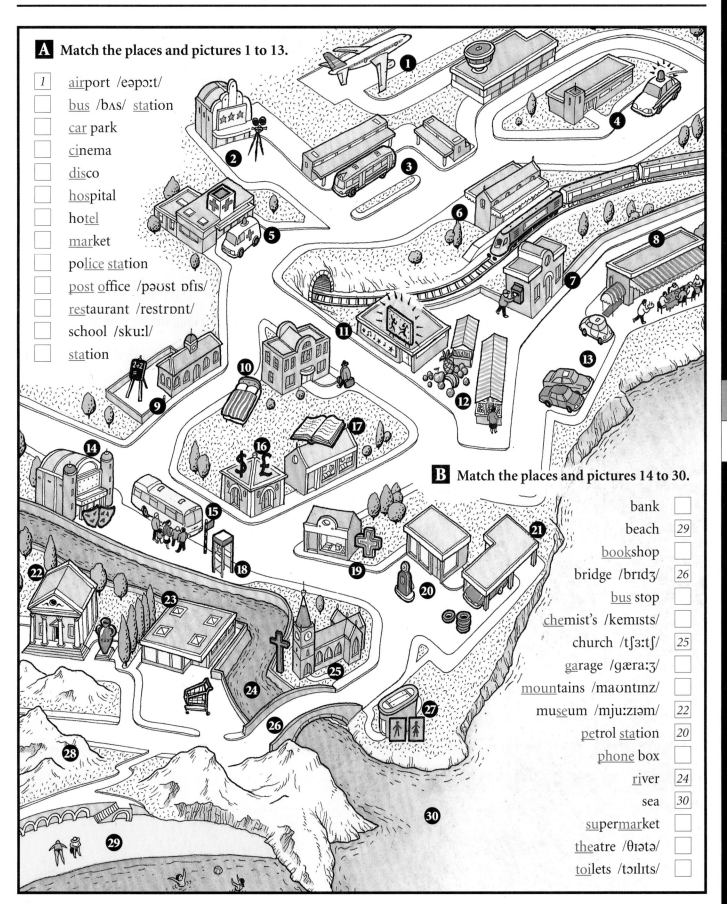

B Match the places and pictures 14 to 30.

bank	
beach	29
bookshop	
bridge /brɪdʒ/	26
bus stop	
chemist's /kemɪsts/	
church /tʃɜːtʃ/	25
garage /gæraːʒ/	
mountains /maʊntɪnz/	
museum /mjuːzɪəm/	22
petrol station	20
phone box	
river	24
sea	30
supermarket	
theatre /θɪətə/	
toilets /tɔɪlɪts/	

4 Small objects

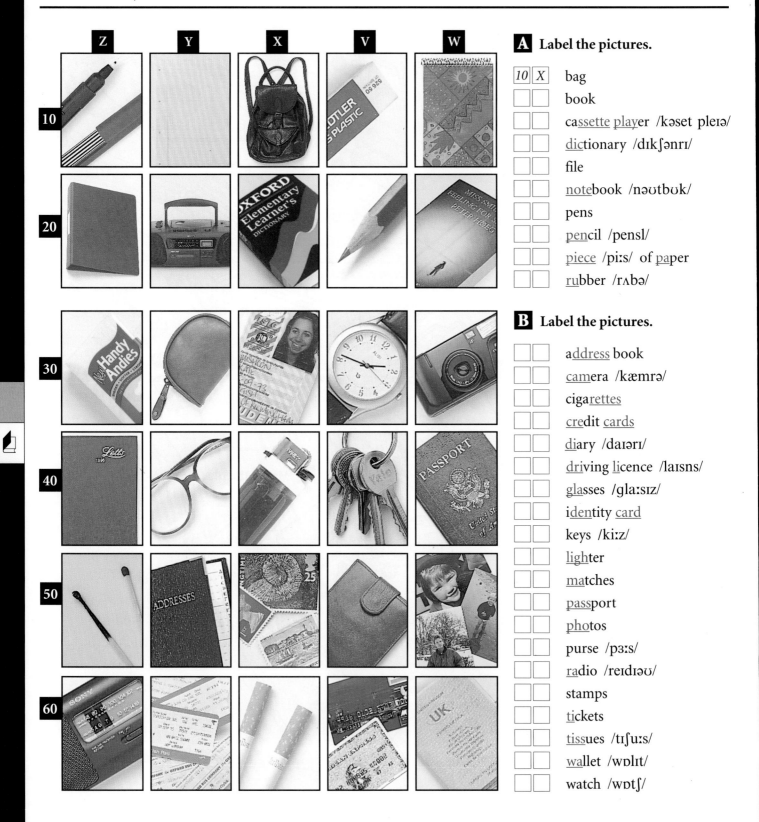

A Label the pictures.

10	X	bag
		book
		cassette player /kəset pleɪə/
		dictionary /dɪkʃənrɪ/
		file
		notebook /nəʊtbʊk/
		pens
		pencil /pensl/
		piece /piːs/ of paper
		rubber /rʌbə/

B Label the pictures.

		address book
		camera /kæmrə/
		cigarettes
		credit cards
		diary /daɪərɪ/
		driving licence /laɪsns/
		glasses /glaːsɪz/
		identity card
		keys /kiːz/
		lighter
		matches
		passport
		photos
10		purse /pɜːs/
		radio /reɪdɪəʊ/
		stamps
		tickets
		tissues /tɪʃuːs/
		wallet /wɒlɪt/
		watch /wɒtʃ/

5 Food and drink

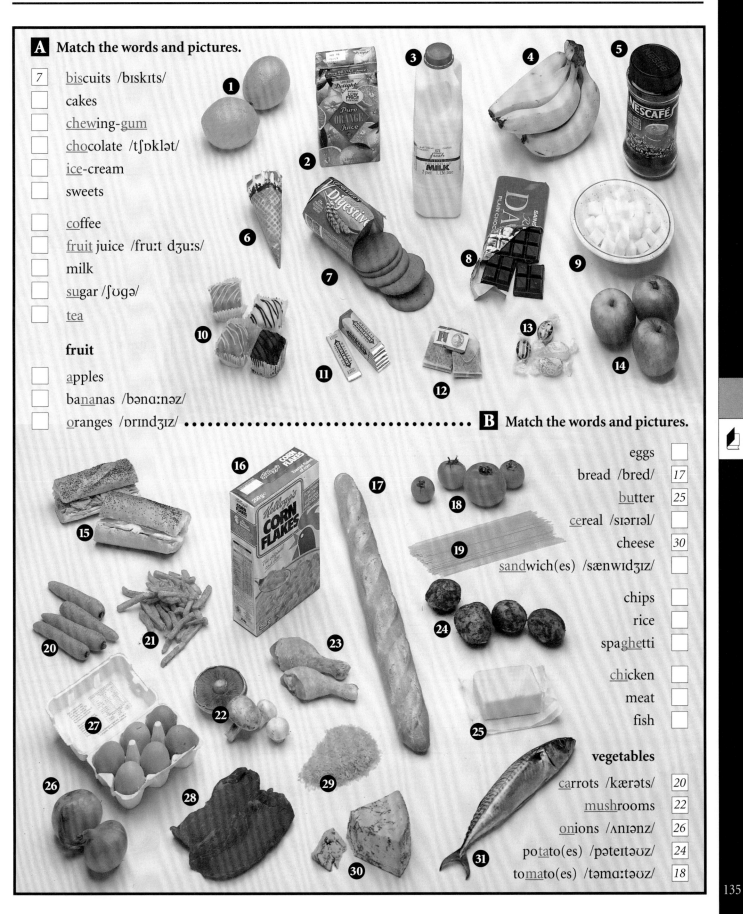

A Match the words and pictures.

7	biscuits /ˈbɪskɪts/
	cakes
	chewing-gum
	chocolate /ˈtʃɒklət/
	ice-cream
	sweets
	coffee
	fruit juice /fruːt dʒuːs/
	milk
	sugar /ˈʃʊgə/
	tea

fruit

	apples
	bananas /bəˈnɑːnəz/
	oranges /ˈɒrɪndʒɪz/

B Match the words and pictures.

eggs	
bread /bred/	17
butter	25
cereal /ˈsɪəriəl/	
cheese	30
sandwich(es) /ˈsænwɪdʒɪz/	
chips	
rice	
spaghetti	
chicken	
meat	
fish	

vegetables

carrots /ˈkærəts/	20
mushrooms	22
onions /ˈʌniənz/	26
potato(es) /pəˈteɪtəʊz/	24
tomato(es) /təˈmɑːtəʊz/	18

6 Time

second /sekənd/

minute /mɪnɪt/

hour /aʊə/

day /deɪ/

week

month

year

last
this
next

century /sentʃʊrɪ/

o'clock /əklɒk/

a quarter /kwɔːtə/ to

a quarter past /pɑːst/

half /hɑːf/ past

Time

at	six o'clock
	midday
	lunchtime
	midnight
	night
	Christmas
	the weekend

B Write the letters.

in	1994
	the 80s

in(the)	sprin☐
	summe☐
	autum☐ /ɔːtəm/
	winte☐

in the	☐orning
	☐fternoon
	☐vening

in	Januar☐y☐ /dʒænjʊərɪ/
of	Februar☐ /febrʊərɪ/
	Marc☐
	Apri☐ /eɪprəl/
	Ma☐
	Jun☐
	Jul☐ /dʒʊlaɪ/
	Augus☐ /ɔːgəst/
	Septembe☐
	Octobe☐
	Novembe☐
	Decembe☐

A Write the letters.

on	Monday /mʌndeɪ/	(the)	1st	first
	☐uesday /tjuːzdeɪ/		2nd	☐econd
	☐ednesday /wenzdeɪ/		3rd	☐hird
	☐hursday /θɜːzdeɪ/		4th	☐ourth
	☐riday /fraɪdeɪ/		5th	☐ifth
	☐aturday /sætədeɪ/		6th	☐ixth
	☐unday /sʌndeɪ/		7th	☐eventh
			8th	☐ighth

yesterday	today
tonight	tomorrow

9th	☐inth
10th	☐enth

C Write the numbers.

11th	eleventh	☐th	eighteenth
☐th	twelfth	19th	☐
13th	thirteenth	☐th	twentieth
☐th	fourteenth	21st	☐
15th	☐	☐nd	twenty-second
☐th	sixteenth	30th	☐
17th	☐	☐st	thirty-first

Happy Birthday !

7 Jobs

Match the jobs and pictures.

7	an actor /æktə/
	a dancer
	a doctor /dɒktə/
	an engineer /endʒɪnɪə/
	a film director
	a fire-fighter
	a footballer
	a manager /mænɪdʒə/
	a police officer
	a taxi-driver
	a teacher
	a waiter

I'm retired. /rɪtaɪəd/

I'm unemployed. /ʌnɪmplɔɪd/

	a civil servant /sɪvl sɜːvənt/
	a dentist
	a flight attendant
	a nurse /nɜːs/
	a pilot /paɪlət/
	a politician /pɒlɪtɪʃn/
	a secretary /sekrətrɪ/
	a shop assistant
	a housewife
	a student /stjuːdnt/

WORD BANK

8 House

A Match the words and pictures 1 to 11.

8	chair
	clock
	desk
	door /dɔː/
	drawer /drɔː/
	floor /flɔː/
11	pictures /pɪktʃəz/
	shelf (shelves)
	table /teɪbl/
	wall /wɔːl/
	window /wɪndəʊ/

B Match the words and pictures 12 to 32.

furniture

	armchair
	bath /bɑːθ/
	bed
	carpet /kɑːpɪt/
	cupboard /kʌbəd/
16	cooker
	fridge /frɪdʒ/
	lamp
15	light
	mirror
	sofa /səʊfə/
	stairs /steəz/

rooms

	bathroom
	bedroom
	dining /daɪnɪŋ/ -room
	garden
	hall
	kitchen /kɪtʃɪn/
	living /lɪvɪŋ/ -room
25	shower /ʃaʊə/
	toilet /tɔɪlɪt/

138

9 Verbs

A Match the verbs and pictures.

8	cook
	dance
	drive
	make *a pizza*
	play *tennis*
	play *the guitar*
	run *five km*
	ski /skiː/
	swim
	use /juːz/ *a computer*

B Match the verbs and pictures.

13	buy /baɪ/ *a newspaper*	18	meet *a friend*		smoke	21	wait *for a bus*
	call *a taxi*		read *a magazine*	16	spend *a lot of money*	30	wash /wɒʃ/ *your hair*
29	clean *the house*	22	relax		study *English*		watch /wɒtʃ/ *TV*
	do *your homework*		see *a film*	12	take *an aspirin*		work /wɜːk/ *for eight hours*
	listen *to music*	20	sleep *for six hours*		tell *a story*		write *a letter*

10 Adjectives

A Match the adjectives and pictures.

big	4	small
cheap		expensive
clean		dirty
easy		difficult
fast /fɑːst/		slow
good		bad
long		short
near		far
new /njuː/		old
nice		horrible
right		wrong
the same		different

B Match the adjectives and pictures.

beautiful /bjuːtɪfl/		ugly
fair		dark
fat		thin
happy		sad
hot		cold
old		young /jʌŋ/
strong		weak
tall		short
		angry
		hungry
		ill
		thirsty
		tired /taɪəd/

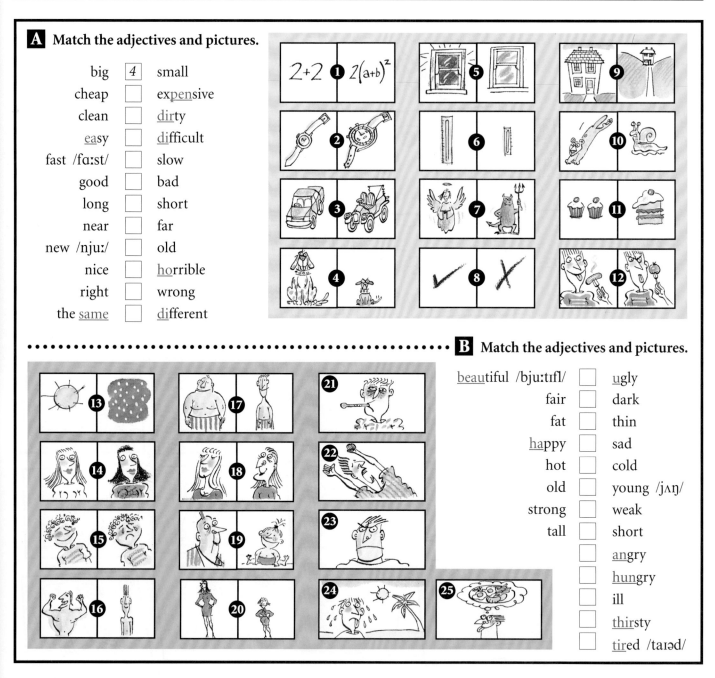

11 Prepositions of place

Match the prepositions and pictures.

	at		near	8
	behind		next to	
	between		on	
	in		on the left	12
	in front of		on the right	4
2	in the middle of		opposite	10
			under	

12 Have, Go, Get

A Match the verbs and pictures.

3	**a** drink
	a (cup of) <u>co</u>ffee
	a <u>sand</u>wich
	a <u>ciga</u>rette
	a <u>show</u>er
	a nice week<u>end</u>! / **a** good time!
	<u>break</u>fast / lunch / <u>din</u>ner

(= have got)

	a car
	children
	long hair / blue eyes

B Match the verbs and pictures.

	home
	<u>sho</u>pping
	<u>swi</u>mming
	out
	away
	to work / school
	to bed
	to the beach
	to the <u>ci</u>nema
	to a <u>res</u>taurant
	for a walk
	by bus / train / plane

C Match the verbs and pictures.

	home
	<u>ma</u>rried
	a <u>ta</u>xi / bus / train
	a fax / <u>le</u>tter
	to work (at 8.00)
	to the <u>sta</u>tion
	up <u>ear</u>ly / late

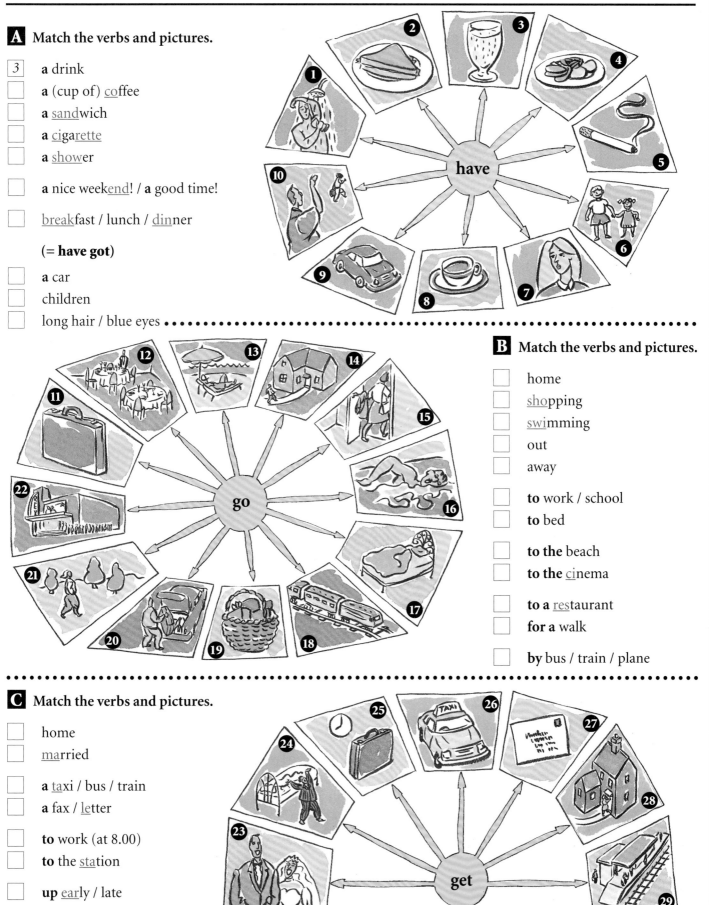

141

13 English sounds

Vowels Look at the pictures. Remember the words. Remember the twenty sounds.

1 fish /fɪʃ/   2 tree /triː/   3 cat /kæt/   4 car /kɑː/
5 clock /klɒk/   6 horse /hɔːs/   7 bull /bʊl/   8 boot /buːt/
9 computer /kəmpˈjuːtə/ 10 bird /bɜːd/   11 egg /eg/   12 up /ʌp/
13 train /treɪn/   14 phone /fəʊn/   15 bike /baɪk/   16 owl /aʊl/
17 boy /bɔɪ/   18 ear /ɪə/   19 chair /tʃeə/   20 tourist /ˈtʊərɪst/

■ short vowels
▪ long vowels
■ diphthongs

Consonants

Look at the pictures. Remember the words. Remember the twenty-four sounds.

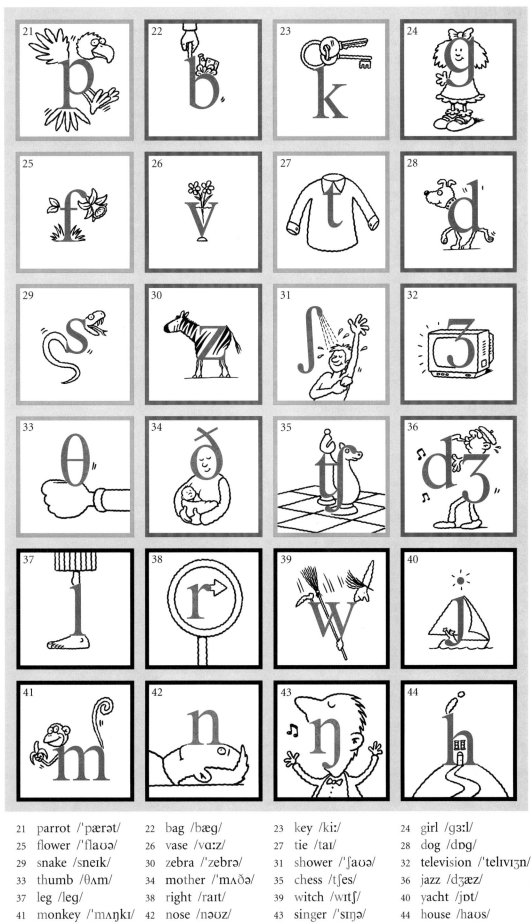

21 parrot /ˈpærət/	22 bag /bæg/	23 key /kiː/	24 girl /gɜːl/
25 flower /ˈflaʊə/	26 vase /vɑːz/	27 tie /taɪ/	28 dog /dɒg/
29 snake /sneɪk/	30 zebra /ˈzebrə/	31 shower /ˈʃaʊə/	32 television /ˈtelɪvɪʒn/
33 thumb /θʌm/	34 mother /ˈmʌðə/	35 chess /tʃes/	36 jazz /dʒæz/
37 leg /leg/	38 right /raɪt/	39 witch /wɪtʃ/	40 yacht /jɒt/
41 monkey /ˈmʌŋkɪ/	42 nose /nəʊz/	43 singer /ˈsɪŋə/	44 house /haʊs/

■ voiced
■ unvoiced

143

16 Irregular verbs

■ Learn and use the top thirty irregular verbs.

Infinitive	Past simple	Example
be (am / is / are)	was / were	Where were you at 6.00? I was in the garden.
break	broke	He broke his leg last year.
buy	bought /bɔːt/	We bought them some flowers.
can	could /kʊd/	Sorry I couldn't come to your party.
come	came	You came home very late last night!
do	did	We did our homework after class.
drive	drove	He drove to Russia in an old BMW.
find	found	I found a wallet in the street.
get	got	They got a taxi home at midnight.
give	gave	She gave him a red rose.
go	went	We went to the beach yesterday.
have	had	She had breakfast in a café.
hear /hɪə/	heard /hɜːd/	I heard a noise outside the window.
leave	left	I left my books at home.
lose /luːz/	lost	I lost my keys last weekend.
make	made	He made a big mistake.
meet	met	They met an old friend on Tuesday.
put /pʊt/	put	She put her purse in her bag.
read /riːd/	read /red/	I read Moby Dick last month.
run	ran	He ran to the ticket office.
say	said /sed/	I said something wrong.
see	saw /sɔː/	We saw an awful film on TV.
send	sent	She sent me a sad letter.
speak	spoke	I spoke to the manager this morning.
spend	spent	We spent a lot of money in Paris.
take	took /tʊk/	I took my car to the garage on Monday.
think	thought /θɔːt/	I thought you were ill.
tell	told	He told me a funny story.
wake up	woke up	I woke up at 4.00 a.m.
write	wrote	She wrote a letter.

■ Learn the verb patterns.

Verb + preposition	Example
agree with	I don't agree with you.
go to	They go to the cinema a lot.
listen to	Don't listen to her.
look at	Look at this photo.
look for	I'm looking for room 13.
speak / talk to	I want to speak / talk to you.
think of	What do you think of Picasso?
wait for	Wait for me, please!
write to	Please write to me!

Verb + infinitive	Example
need to	I need to learn English for my job.
want to	We want to go to Brazil next summer.
like to	Would you like to have dinner with us?

Verb + (verb)-ing	Example
hate	I hate shopping.
like	She doesn't like flying.
love	He loves cooking.